THE SAYINGS

OF

G·O·D

COMPILED AND TRANSLATED BY
YEHOSHUA PERSKY

JASON ARONSON INC.
Northvale, New Jersey
London

Design: Ernie Haim

Library of Congress Cataloging-in-Publication Data

Bible. O.T. Pentateuch. English. Persky. Selections. 1990.
    The sayings of God / compiled and translated by
      Yehoshua Persky.
      p.   cm.
    Includes index.
    ISBN 0-87668-796-6
    1. God—Biblical teaching. I. Persky, Yehoshua. II. Title.
BS1192.6.B5313   1990
222'.105209—dc20   90-37555
                                        CIP

Manufactured in the United States of America.
Jason Aronson Inc. offers books and cassettes.
For information and catalog write to Jason Aronson Inc.,
230 Livingston Street, Northvale, New Jersey 07647.

In Memory
of
My Beloved Grandparents
Benjamin and Ethel Persky
Victor and Jenny Bernstein

CONTENTS

CONTENTS

FOREWORD

SPEECH—MAN'S MARK OF DIVINITY

Only three beings in the biblical universe share abstract speech—God, man, and angels (Bilaam's donkey is a one-time exception). In the first story of Creation, God appears only with the name *Elohim*, the Lord of Nature (in Jewish tradition, Hebrew letters have numerical equivalents—*gematria*; the Bible yields hidden or additional meanings by exploring alternative words or concepts that have similar totals to the *gematria* in a given set of letters, words, verses, etc.; in *gematria*, *Elohim* = 86 = *Hateva*, Nature). As such, God creates man with the potential of developing within himself an image of the Lord of Nature (Genesis 1:26). Man can understand natural law, enabling him to control and manipulate all existence. Rashi, however, the most famous Jewish Bible commentator, in the second account of Creation (Genesis 2:7), describes man only as a *speaking* being, one who has and expresses deep personal knowledge. Only then does God appear in His infinite relational Essence, *Adonoi Elohim*, and only then does man begin to speak. Rashi, agreeing with ancient Aramaic translations of the text, says that "Man became a truly alive soul" means that "Man became a speaking soul."

"If you speak, remember that this power comes from your soul, a part of God. Even mundane, secular Hebrew speech uses the letters of the Holy *aleph-bet*—brings their innate holiness back to its Source, connects all reality to God" (Baal Shem Tov, *Keter Shem Tov* 31).

One should strive to avoid anything off-color or disgusting in his speech (*Pesachim* 3a; Leviticus *Rabbah* 24). "There are three partners in man (father, mother, and God)—God gives him his spirit, soul, and the speech of his mouth" (*Niddah* 31a).

Maimonides believed that astral bodies possess superhuman intelligence and endurance (*Mishneh Torah, Yesodei Hatorah* 3:9): "All stars and heavenly spheres have souls, knowledge, and understanding—they are alive and recognize 'He who spoke and the universe was!' Each, according to its greatness and rank, praises and glorifies [its] Creator, as do the angels. Just as they recognize the Holy One, Blessed be He, so they possess awareness of themselves and the angels above them." Although they praise and glorify God, theirs is a silent speech: "The Heavens proclaim the glory of the Lord and the firmament declares the work of His hands. . . . There is no speech, there are no words . . ." (Psalm 19). Indeed, Rambam clearly states that angels are not composed of matter, their wings but a metaphor for their elusive fleeting nature; thus they are higher than astral bodies (*Guide of the Perplexed* I:49, II:6,7).

In *Mishneh Torah, Yesodei Hatorah* 4:8, Rambam describes human uniqueness, man's Divine Image, as his superior intelligence, sometimes called *nefesh* (soul), sometimes *ruach* (spirit). Man has an intelligent soul, which knows and apprehends idealistic beings, pure forms devoid of matter, for example, angels. This soul is neither a composite of biological matter nor a product of biological drives, but comes directly from God in Heaven. The form of the soul is thus independent of the body and survives death to endure forever: "And the dust shall return to the earth, as it once was, and the spirit shall return to the Lord Who gave it" (Ecclesiastes 12:7). Unlike Rashi, Rambam does not mention speech as such, either here or in his description of man in *Guide of the Perplexed* I:1. So in describing prayer, he alludes to a higher state where thoughts are not externalized. This may reflect both his general disdain of the physical aspects of man and his disputed denial of the corporeality of God.

So the Kotzker Rebbe said that silence is the loudest cry and a broken heart the greatest wholeness. "Sometimes one is silent and receives reward for the silence, sometimes he speaks and receives reward for the speech" (*Zevahim* 115b). "All my days I grew up among the wise and found nothing better for the body than silence. All who multiply words bring sin in their wake" (R. Shimon b. Gamaliel, *Avot* 1).

Rav Nachman of Braslav expresses the opposite view, that talk is the vessel through which God's abundance is received; hence, prayer must be articulated in words, not just thought. Jewish law indeed states that a thought does not have the legal effect of a statement (*Berachot* 20b). Words that remain in the heart are not considered words (*Kiddushin* 49b). By giving verbal utterance to inner knowledge, one actually clarifies and increases it (Song of Songs *Rabbah* 1:7 on Proverbs 16:23).

Speech, per Torah, is not merely a means of conveying information, it projects and exposes one's soul, one's deepest and most sensitive perceptions. It externalizes the inner soul of man, bringing Divinity into the physical world. As such, its quality and impact are in proportion to the speaker's depth of soul. Thus the rabbinic dictum: Words that emit from the heart, enter the heart.

Yitzchak Chayutman sees The Word as the theme of all five books of the Pentateuch, reflected in their Hebrew names. The first book of the Torah, Genesis, *B'reisheet*, "In the Beginning," begins with only God's word and no human audience. Man then emulates God, as he names everything, culminating in Exodus, *V'Aleh Sh'mot*, the Book of Names. God calls to man in Leviticus, *Vayikra*, the Book of Calling, of commandments. Man's response, his trial run in living according to the Torah, is the Book of Numbers, *Bamidbar*, literally "in speaking" or "in the place where one cannot speak." Finally, Deuteronomy, *Davarim*, "Words," is the merging of the speech of Moshe and God.

Judaism stresses the Oral Tradition, direct contact with the speech and soul of a master of Moshe's tradition, far beyond mere study of a book. It was even forbidden to write down the Oral Tradition, until its survival required it (*Gittin* 60b). All reality is created by Divine Utterances, combinations of Hebrew letters (Genesis 1). With the word of God, the heavens were made (Psalm 33:6; cf. *Shabbat* 119b) . . . "not by labor or toil, but only by a word, says R. Judah b. R. Shimon" (Genesis *Rabbah* 32). Some, however, like Rambam, understand the Divine Word as meaning Divine Thought and Intention (see *Otzar Yisroel, Dibbur*). Man's inner reality is later recreated via God's Ten Utterances at Sinai. Man's own words can have similar impact, insofar as he has developed his own Divine Essence. "A righteous man decrees and God makes it come true" (*Shabbat* 59b, quoting Job 22:28). Yaakov states that whoever stole Lavan's idols shall die (not knowing that it was Rachel [Genesis 11:32]). Rashi says that Rachel died shortly thereafter as a result of his words, albeit contrary to his intention.

Only if great teachers personified their own teachings, if their words reflected their selves, were their maxims taught. It is much easier to talk beautifully than to live beautifully. *Avot* 6 opens, "The sages taught . . . blessed is he who chose *them* and *their teaching*." The personal status of the teacher comes first. "Words are beautiful when they emit from the mouth of he who performs them" (Tosefta, *Yevamot* 8). Hence, one who attributes a quotation to its creator brings redemption to the world (*Megillah* 15a). Moshe reaches man's ultimate capability. Almost the entire book of Deuteronomy is spoken by Moses, God only adding a bit on His own. God includes Moshe's words (Moshe's *Mishnah*) in His Torah, beginning the Oral Law Process (Abarbanel). Conversely, when speech is used destructively, to dim Divinity in the world, to build a Tower of Babel, God destroys it: "The whole earth was of one language (Hebrew, according to Rashi) and unified speech. . . . God said . . . 'Come, let us go down and there confound their language, that they may not understand one another's speech'" (Genesis 11).

Esther wants her tale to become part of Holy Writ, "words of Peace and Truth" (Esther 9:30). For speech to be truly sacred, it must contain and reconcile these two seemingly contradictory forces: where there is (absolute insistence upon) truth, there is no peace (each person sees truth differently) and they will be fighting constantly; and where there is (absolute insistence upon) peace, there is no truth (for fear of unpleasant relationships). We pray for their eventual union: "When loving-kindness and truth have met together, then righteousness and peace have kissed each other" (Psalm 85:11). Often, when somebody tells the truth, he is persecuted and shunned. When people accept that the greatest kindness is the disclosure of truth, then all will occupy their truthful and just places in the Divine Scheme, bringing true peace and harmony (Rav S. R. Hirsch: "These are the things you shall do—each man should proclaim truth with his neighbor; truth and a judgment of peace you shall adjudicate in your gates" (Zechariah 8:16).

The holiness of speech entails its truth and fulfillment. Moshe spoke to the tribal heads of the children of Israel saying: "This is what God has ordered [you to oversee]: When a man vows a vow to God or swears an oath to forbid something to himself, he shall not profane his word; *he shall act in accordance with all that left his mouth* (Numbers 30:2–3). Judaism discourages those voluntary commitments unlikely to be fulfilled, for example, conversion: "Better that you not vow, rather than vow and not pay" (Ecclesiastes 5:3–4). "If you refrain from vowing, there will be no sin in you" (Deuteronomy 23:23). "Think before acting—avoid impulsive vows. Indeed, God never retracts His promise for good, even if it is conditional and the condition is not fulfilled" (*Berachot* 7a).

Truth is a common biblical and rabbinic topic, for example, "The seal of the Holy One, Blessed be He, is Truth" (*Shabbat* 55a). "God the Lord is Truth" (Jeremiah 10:10). "Your Torah is Truth" (Psalm 119:142). "The Rabbis fully endorsed the biblical demand for man uncompromisingly to

honor his word, whether accompanied by a vow or not. . . . 'Let thy yea
be yea, and thy nay be nay.' He who changes his word commits as heavy
a sin as he who worships idols" (*Sanhedrin* 92a); "he who utters an untruth is
excluded from the Divine Presence" (Hertz Pentateuch, p. 730, cf. political
life).

Sages may annul vows if no one else is affected; misapprehensions may
have originally engendered the vow. The famous public annulment, *Kol
Nidre*, starts the Yom Kippur liturgy; Hirsch opposed its continuation. It was
originally instituted to negate the vows forced upon Jews by Islam and
Christianity; they killed Jews who denied that God changed His mind
about His covenantal Pentateuch.

Even harmless lies are forbidden (see Jeremiah 9:4); a God-aware man
will keep even a promise made only in his heart: "And speaks the truth in
his heart" (Psalm 15:2). One must not claim credit for that which he has not
done; a heathen also may not be misled (*Menorat Hamaor* II 2:2). Faith entails
the obligation to love truth, from which it stems; unfailing truth makes
one's prayers heard and brings him close to God, granting "life in the world
to come" (Psalm 145:18). Israel is the nation most inclined to follow Torah,
called truth (Proverbs 23:23). A redeemed Israel will exemplify truth: "The
remnant of Israel shall not do iniquity nor speak lies; neither shall a
deceitful tongue be found in their mouth" (Zechariah 3:13; cf. 8:16; *Kad
Hakemach*).

The search for truth is the essence of talmudic process. Medieval
scholars insisted on reconciling reason and revelation. Prophets refused to
ascribe to God traits that they did not experience (*Yoma* 69b; L. Jacobs,
What Does Judaism Say About . . . ?). My son, Ariel Fogelman, asked if a
child who does not want to learn should pray to learn; I replied that he
should pray to *want* to learn! But does he want to want? I would answer,
"Deep down, yes!"

Some Chassidic Thoughts on Truth

"Pure truth doesn't exist in this world. One may be very far from
falsehood, but no one is altogether truthful" (the Kossover Rebbe).

"From a false word, you will be far" (Exodus 23:7)—"from God, who
despises falsehood" (the Sassover Rebbe, Menorat Zahav, Mishpatim).

"Everything in the world can be imitated except truth. Truth that is
imitated is not [ultimate] truth" (the Kotzker Rebbe).

Find your own unique approach to God and Torah, don't just ape your
parents and teachers. The search for truth and integrity must itself be
peaceful; it must not become a war against those whose similar search leads
them elsewhere.

Moshe Kohn quotes R. Nachman of Braslav: "Truth cannot tolerate triumphalism. If victory is what you are after, you cannot arrive at truth." Following Kabbalah, R. Nachman described Noach's Ark as a symbol for The Word (both, in Hebrew, called *tavah*), the corruption of which was the original cause of the world's decadence and destruction. Everyone must strive to make his speech a vehicle for holiness—a "window in the ark"; some such windows are as a brilliant diamond, seemingly emitting its own radiance; others are not so creative, but their word can still be as a glass window, transmitting the creativity of others, their teachers. Truth is acquired by cleaving to the righteous while separating from the unpious— not via reason, that is, negative emotions impede truthful perception unless one absorbs the mindset of another who transcends such feelings. (R. Nachman banned rational works such as Maimonides' *Guide*, Ibn Ezra, and Radak from his followers—try reasoning with a Braslaver.)

Rav Nachman equates truth with unity, Divinity, and strength. If truth prevailed, the world's problems would disappear. Flattery leads to false- hood. Where there is no truth, there is no true kindness and peace. Truth leads to fame. Quarrels of children stem from untruthful parents. Those who fear others, lacking self-confidence, lie, forgetting the fear of God; they who resist falsehood usually conquer their adversaries (e.g., Sharansky, Rambam, Ramchal).

R. Yisroel of Rizhin compared God's preferred altar of mother earth (Exodus 20:24) to the most pleasing altar of silence; if one must speak, build an "altar of lifeless stones"—they should at least be "unhewn" (Exodus 20:25), honest and direct, not stylized.

The Lubliner Rebbe professed his greater love for the wicked man who knows it than for the righteous man who knows it—the former is truthful and God loves truth; the latter is untruthful, as everyone has some sin. God hates falsity!

The Tchernobler Rebbe urged one who has lied to proclaim, "I just told a lie," a consciousness-raising remedy.

Words of Peace

Truth is not everything. Not all that should be thought should be uttered and not all that should be uttered should be printed. The Rizhiner Rebbe noted that talk can cause greater tribulations than a tempestuous wind (cf. Amos 4:13); one must carefully consider the effects of his words. Rav Nachman predicts physical, intellectual, and spiritual poverty for the person who speaks worthless and malicious words, which also pollute the air and damage the soul of those who listen to them. Conversely, holy talk, words of prayer and Torah, can pull one up from the lowest depths. "A person should always admit to truth and proclaim the truth *in his heart* [from the Prayer Book]." One should *omit* a truthful fact when someone's feelings may be hurt by it, so God skips Sarah's mention of Avraham's aging when repeating her words to him (Genesis 18:12–13). A truncated account is not really a true one.

One may even make up a story to avoid fighting, as Yaakov's sons did. They told Yosef that Yaakov had commanded him to forgive them (Genesis 50:16f). We know of no such command, although Yaakov would have said it. God commands such conduct (R. Natan on 1 Samuel 16:2). Peace may represent higher truths, unity and love, transcending "truths" of detail in a world of illusion. God's Creation, via utterances, is "very good." Our words must not only result in truth, but also in goodness and benefit; even true slander is forbidden. The Talmud permits lying to deny one's great scholarship, in answer to questions about one's intimate life, and to discourage others from taking advantage of a generous host (*Baba Metzia* 23b–24a). The Koretzer Rebbe said that we must exercise quality control over our words; not only must they be true, but they must be devoid of anger and flattery. Words of anger, the highest impurity, can only cause others to add to their sin.

Lack of truth and peace caused the respective destructions of the two Temples. Torah, the only source of ultimate truth, was missing from the first Temple society; for peace and harmony with their neighbors, Jews adopted perverse idolatry—their slogan was "Peace! Peace!"; men of truth were considered troublemakers. Children slipping away from Torah and the bad influence of their friends and relatives are ignored in the name of peace. Do we so ignore our monetary interests in the name of peaceful relations? False prophets identify their compromise truth with the ancient truth. Peace must not preclude war against falseness.

The second Temple period had much Torah truth, but lacked peace—everyone harbored groundless hatred for his fellow. People fought to be chief rabbi. "Torah Truth" concealed a search for egotistical power and prestige. The corruption of human nature leads to alienation from mother nature. The Jew mourns and fasts for three weeks amid summer beauty, for the loss of political freedom (17th of Tamuz) and the destruction of our spiritual center (9th of Av). One day her fasts will be turned to summer rejoicing—nature again in harmony with man—when the Jews will *love* both truth and peace (Zechariah 8:19); only then can the third Temple arise and remain (Hirsch).

There is no exact formula for balancing truth and peace; Moshe stressed truth and Aharon peace. Midrashim say that Aharon would lie to an enemy, claiming that each really liked the other and was sorry for their fight—this would bring them back together. Yet his tremendous desire for peace almost destroyed Israel when he cooperated with the makers of the Golden Calf.

Even man's greatest insights and reactions are far removed from those of God: "Do not trust in Princes, in the son of man who holds no salvation" (Psalm 146). God's model Word is active and creative, not just informative: *"As rain and snow descend from Heaven, not to return there without watering the earth, giving birth and growth . . . so shall My word be, which leaves My mouth; it won't return to Me empty, unless it's done what I wished and benefited he to whom I sent it"* (Isaiah 55). When we study the Bible, God's Word, we experience Him; indeed, the Jerusalem Talmud (*Peah* 1) states that (the reward for performing) all of the commandments of the Torah does not equal (the reward for studying) one word of the Torah.

Every single word that left God's mouth appears in seventy forms of expression, as sparks emitting from the anvil. Each such word has two crowns and fills the entire universe with fragrance (*Shabbat* 88b). Each word of God itself creates an angel (*Haggigah* 14a). It is reasonable to assume that those statements that He attributes to Himself especially reflect His essence and our lives, that they are the highest blend of truth and peace. Persky is owed a debt for bringing them to our attention in such a convenient form. May we all be enlightened as we read them and meditate upon them.

Rebbe Zusia of Hanipoli was a disciple of the Maggid of Mezritch, but he never absorbed a lecture! The Maggid would begin his lectures with a verse: "God said. . . ." As soon as Rebbe Zusia heard these two words from the holy Man, he became so rapturous, so ecstatic that God indeed spoke to man, he didn't hear the rest of the lecture. When he left the yeshiva, the Maggid said that he had learned more than anyone else.

Yakov Fogelman

IN THE BEGINNING GOD CREATED
THE HEAVEN AND THE EARTH.

And the earth was formless and void, and darkness was on
the face of the deep. And the spirit of God hovered over the
surface of the waters.

AND GOD SAID . . .

GENESIS

*T*here will be light.

◇   ◇   ◇

*T*here will be a sky amidst the waters. There will be a separation between water and water.

Genesis 1:6

◇   ◇   ◇

*T*he waters below the heavens will converge to one place. The dry land will appear.

Genesis 1:9

◇   ◇   ◇

*T*he earth will sprout grass, herb seeding seed, fruit tree yielding fruit of its kind, with its seed in it, on the land.

Genesis 1:11

◇   ◇   ◇

*T*here will be luminaries in the arc of the heavens to distinguish between the day and the night. They will be for signs, for seasons, for days,

◆ 1 ◆

and for years. The luminaries in the arc of the heavens will illuminate the earth.

Genesis 1:14–15

*T*he waters will be infested by swarming, living, creatures; and fowl will fly above the earth across the arc of the sky.

Genesis 1:20

*B*e fruitful and multiply, and fill the water in the seas; and fowl will multiply on the earth.

Genesis 1:22

*T*he earth will bring forth living beings of their kinds: beast, creeper, and land-animal of their kind.

Genesis 1:24

*W*e will make man in our image, in our likeness, to rule over the fish of the sea, over the fowl of the heavens, over the beasts, over the entire earth, and over everything that creeps on the ground.

Genesis 1:26

*B*e fruitful and multiply, and fill the earth, and subdue her. Rule over the fish of the sea, over the fowl of the heavens, and over every animal which creeps on the earth.

Genesis 1:28

*H*ere, I have given to you every herb bearing seed which is on the face of the entire earth, and every tree on which is fruit bearing seed: to you it will be for food. For every animal of the earth, and for every fowl of the heaven, and for every creeper on the earth in which is a living soul, all green herbage is for food.

Genesis 1:29–30

*Y*ou may eat food from every tree in the garden, but you may not eat from the tree of the knowledge of good and evil, because on the day when you eat from it, you must die.

Genesis 2:16–17

*I*t is not good that the man is alone. I will make a helpmate for him.

Genesis 2:18

*W*here are you?

Genesis 3:9

*W*ho told you that you are naked? Have you eaten from the tree from which I commanded you not to eat?

Genesis 3:11

◇ ◇ ◇

*W*hat is this you have done?

Genesis 3:13

◇ ◇ ◇

*B*ecause you have done this, you are more cursed than every other beast and every other animal of the field. You will go on your belly, and you will eat dust all the days of your life. I will set hostility between you and woman, between your seed and her seed. Man will strike your head, and you will strike his heel.

Genesis 3:14–15

◇ ◇ ◇

I will greatly increase your labor and toil. You will bear children with travail. And your desire will be for your husband, and he will rule over you.

Genesis 3:16

◇ ◇ ◇

*B*ecause you listened to the voice of your wife and ate from the tree of which I commanded you, saying: "Do not eat from it," cursed is the ground for your sake. You will eat from it with toil all the days of your life, and it will grow thorns and thistles for you, and you will eat the herb of the field. You will eat bread by the sweat of your brow, until you return to the ground, because from it you were taken. For you are dust, and to dust you will return.

Genesis 3:17–19

*N*ow the man has become like one of us, knowing good and evil. And now, perhaps, he will reach to take from the tree of life as well and will eat and live forever.

Genesis 3:22

*W*hy are you angry? And why are you downcast? Surely, if you do good, there is forgiveness; and if you do not do good, sin crouches at the door. To you is its desire, yet you may control it.

Genesis 4:6–7

*W*here is Abel your brother?

Genesis 4:9

*W*hat have you done? The voice of the blood of your brother cries to me from the ground. Now then, you are cursed by the ground which has opened its mouth to take the blood of your brother from your hand. When you work the land, it will no longer give you its strength. You are to be a wanderer and a nomad on the earth.

Genesis 4:10–12

*F*rom now on, anyone who kills Cain will be avenged sevenfold.

Genesis 4:15

My spirit will not reside in man forever, as he is also flesh. Therefore his days are to be a hundred and twenty years.

Genesis 6:3

◇   ◇   ◇

I will wipe man, whom I have created, off the face of the earth: man, beast, creeper, and the fowl of the heavens, because I regret having made them.

Genesis 6:7

◇   ◇   ◇

The end of all flesh has come before me, because the earth is full of man's violence. Therefore, I will now destroy man along with the earth. Make yourself a gopher-wood ark. Make the ark with rooms, and tar it inside and outside with tar. And this is how you are to make it: the length of the ark, three hundred forearms; its width, fifty forearms; and its height, thirty forearms. Make a window above for the ark, and finish it to a forearm. And put the opening of the ark on the side. Make it with second and third sub-levels. And now I will bring the flood-water on the earth to destroy all flesh, in which is the spirit of life, from under the heavens. Everything on the earth will perish. Yet, I will establish my contract with you; and you will come to the ark, you and your sons, and your wife, and your sons' wives with you. And from all life, of all flesh, you are to bring with you two of each to the ark to keep alive. They are to be male and female. Two of each, the fowl with its mate, the beast with its mate, and every creeper of the ground with its mate are to come to you to to live. Therefore, you are to take from every food which is eaten and gather it to yourself. It is to be for you and for them for food.

Genesis 6:13–21

◇   ◇   ◇

Come, you and all your house, to the ark, because I have seen you as righteous before me in this generation. Take to yourself of all the pure beasts, seven of each—a male and its female; and of the beasts which are not pure, two—a male and its female; also, of the fowl of heaven, seven of each—male and female, to keep alive their seed on the face of the entire earth. Because, in seven more days, I will make it rain on the earth for forty days and forty nights, and I will destroy every living thing which I have made from off the face of the earth.

Genesis 7:1–4

Go out from the ark, you and your wife, your sons, and your sons' wives with you. Take out with you every animal which has been with you, of all flesh—of fowl, of beast, and of everything which creeps on the earth—so they may breed on the earth and be fruitful and multiply on the earth.

Genesis 8:16–17

I will never again curse the ground for man's sake, because the inclination of man's heart is evil from his youth. And I will never again strike all life, as I have done. All the remaining days of the earth, sowing and harvest, autumn and spring, summer and winter, day and night, will not cease.

Genesis 8:21–22

Be fruitful and multiply and fill the earth. Fear of you and terror of you will be upon every animal of the earth, upon every fowl of the heavens, upon everything which creeps on the ground, and upon every fish of the sea. They are given into your hands. Every living creature is food for you, as is the green herb. I have given you everything, but you may not eat flesh with living blood.

Genesis 9:1–4

And yet, I will avenge the blood of your souls. I will avenge it from the hand of every animal. I will avenge the soul of man from the hand of man—from the hand of man's brother. He who sheds the blood of man, his blood will be shed by man, because man was made in the image of God. So you, be fruitful and multiply, abound on the earth and multiply on it.

Genesis 9:5–7

And I, here, will establish my contract with you and with your descendants after you, and with every living being which is with you: with fowl, with beast, and with every animal of the earth which is with you, from everything which goes out of the ark to every animal of the earth. I will establish my contract with you: that all flesh will never again be cut off by the waters of the flood, and there will never again be a flood to destroy the earth.

Genesis 9:9–11

*T*his is the sign which I give of the contract between me and you and every living being which is with you, for everlasting generations: I have set my rainbow in a cloud, and it will be a sign of the contract between me and the earth. Hence, it will be that when I cover the earth with clouds, the rainbow will be seen in a cloud, and I will remember my contract which is between me and you and every living soul in all flesh, and the waters will never again flood to destroy all flesh. Therefore, the rainbow will be in the cloud, and I will see it to remember the everlasting contract between God and every living soul in all flesh which is on the earth.

Genesis 9:12–16

*T*his is the sign of the contract I have established between me and all flesh on earth.

Genesis 9:17

*H*ere, one people and one language to all, and this they begin to build (the Tower of Babel)! And now, they will not be prevented from anything they contrive to do. Come, let us descend there and confuse their language, so a man will not understand his fellow-man's language.

Genesis 11:6–7

*G*o from your land, from your birthplace, and from your father's house, to the land which I will show you. Then, will I make of you a great nation, and I will bless you and make your name great, and you will be a blessing. I will bless them who bless you and curse them who curse you; and all the families of the land will be blessed in you.

Genesis 12:1–3

◇   ◇   ◇

I will give this land to your descendants.

Genesis 12:7

*N*ow, raise your eyes, and from the place where you are, look northward, southward, eastward, and westward, because I will give to you and to your descendants, forever, all the land which you see. I will make your descendants as the dust of the earth, so that if a man is about to count the dust of the earth, also your descendants he may count. Arise, walk in the land, to its length and to its width, because I will give it to you.

Genesis 13:14–17

*F*ear not, Abram. I am a shield to you! Your merit is very great.

Genesis 15:1

*T*his (Ishmael) will not be your heir, because he who comes out of your loins will be your heir.

Genesis 15:4

*N*ow, look heavenwards and count the stars—if you can count them. So (numerous) will be your descendants.

Genesis 15:5

I am the Eternal who brought you out of Ur Kasdim to give you this land as an inheritance.

Genesis 15:7

*T*ake a three-year-old heifer for me, a three-year-old goat, a three-year-old ram, a dove and a young pigeon.

Genesis 15:9

*Y*ou must know that your descendants will be strangers in a land not theirs and will serve them (the Egyptians) and submit to them for four hundred years. Yet, I will also judge the nation which they (your descendants) will serve, and afterwards they will leave with great wealth.

However, you will join your ancestors in peace. You will be buried at a good old age. Then, a fourth generation will return here, because the wickedness of the Amorite is not yet complete.

Genesis 15:13–16

I have given this land to your descendants: from the river of Egypt until the great river, the river Perath—of the Kenite, of the Kenizzite, of the Kadmonite, of the Hittite, of the Perizzite, of the Rephaim, of the Amorite, of the Canaanite, of the Girgashite, and of the Jebusite.

Genesis 15:18–21

*H*agar, handmaid of Sarai, from where have you come? And where will you go?

Genesis 16:8

*R*eturn to your mistress, and submit to her.

Genesis 16:9

*I*ndeed, I will multiply your descendants. Then will they be an innumerable multitude.

Genesis 16:10

*N*ow you are pregnant and will bear a son. You are to name him Ishmael, because the Eternal has heard your suffering. However, he will be a wild man—his hand against all; and everyone's hands against him. And he will dwell among all his brothers.

Genesis 16:11–12

I am God Almighty. Walk before me and be perfect. Then, I will grant my contract between me and you, and I will multiply you very greatly.

Genesis 17:1–2

*B*ehold, my contract is with you. You will be a father to many nations. Your name will no longer be called Abram, but your name will be Abraham, because I have made you a father of many nations. Therefore, I will make you very, very fruitful and will make you into nations, and kings will emerge from you. I will establish my contract, between me and you and your descendants after you, in their generations, as an everlasting contract, to be God to you and to your descendants after you. I will give the land of your wanderings, the whole land of Canaan, as an everlasting portion to you and to your descendants after you. I will be God to them.

Genesis 17:4–8

*Y*ou are to safeguard my contract, you and your descendants after you, throughout their generations. This is my contract, between me and you and your descendants after you, which you will safeguard: Every male among you is to be circumcised. You are to circumcise the flesh of your foreskin. It will be as a sign of the contract between me and you. You are to circumcise every male among you at eight days old, throughout your generations, house-born, or money-bought from any foreigner, who is not of your descendants. Your house-born and your money-bought must be circumcised, so my contract will be in your flesh as an everlasting contract. As for an uncircumcised male who does not circumcise the flesh of his foreskin, his soul will be cut off from his people—he has breached my contract.

Genesis 17:9–14

*S*arai, your wife, do not call her name Sarai, because Sarah is her name. I will bless her, and I will also give you a son from her. I will bless her, and she will become nations. Kings of peoples will come from her.

Genesis 17:15–16

*Y*et, Sarah, your wife, will bear you a son, and you are to call his name Isaac. I will establish my contract with him as an everlasting contract for his descendants after him. And as for Ishmael, I have heard you. Here, I will bless him and make him fruitful and multiply him very greatly. He will beget twelve princes. I will make him into a large nation, but I will establish my contract with Isaac, whom Sarah will bear for you, at this season, in the coming year.

Genesis 17:19–21

◇　◇　◇

Do so, as you have said.

Genesis 18:5

◇　◇　◇

Where is Sarah your wife?

Genesis 18:9

◇　◇　◇

Indeed, I will return to you at the right time, and then—a son for Sarah your wife.

Genesis 18:10

◇　◇　◇

Why did Sarah laugh at this, saying, "But, having grown old, will I truly bear?" Is anything too wondrous for the Eternal? I will return to you at the right time and season, and for Sarah—a son.

Genesis 18:13

◇　◇　◇

No, because you laughed.

Genesis 18:15

◇　◇　◇

Should I conceal from Abraham what I will do—when Abraham will indeed become a great and mighty nation, and all the nations of the world will be blessed in him? For I know him, that he will command his children and his house after him to safeguard the way of the Eternal—to do charity and justice, in order for the Eternal to bring upon Abraham that which he has spoken of him.

Genesis 18:17–19

*B*ecause the cry of Sodom and Gomorrah is great, and because their sin is very heavy, I will descend now and see: if they have caused the cry coming to me—annihilation! If not, I will know.

Genesis 18:20–21

*I*f I should find in Sodom, inside the city, fifty charitable men, I will bear with the entire place for their sakes.

Genesis 18:26

*I*f I should find forty and five there, I will not destroy it.

Genesis 18:28

*F*or the sake of forty, I will not do it.

Genesis 18:29

*I*f I should find thirty there, I will not do it.

Genesis 18:30

*F*or the sake of the twenty, I will not destroy it.

Genesis 18:31

*F*or the sake of the ten, I will not destroy it.

Genesis 18:32

*N*o, for we will spend the night in the street.

Genesis 19:2

*W*hom else do you have here? Your son-in-law, your sons, and your daughters, and all that you have in the city—bring out from this place, because we will destroy this place. Because their cry has grown before the Eternal, the Eternal has sent us to destroy it.

Genesis 19:12–13

*G*et up! Take your wife and your two remaining daughters, or you will perish in the wickedness of the city.

Genesis 19:15

*E*scape for your soul! Do not look behind you! And do not stand anywhere in the valley! Escape to the mountain or you will perish.

Genesis 19:17

*H*ere, I will also show you favor in this: that I will not overthrow the city of which you have spoken. Quickly, escape there, because I cannot do anything until you get there.

Genesis 19:21–22

*N*ow you will die because of the woman whom you took, because she is the wife of a husband.

Genesis 20:3

I also know that you did this in the innocence of your heart, and also that I restrained you from sinning against me. Therefore, I did not let you touch her. Now then, return the man's wife, because he is a prophet and will pray on your behalf, and you will live. However, if you do not return her, know that you must die—you and all that is yours.

Genesis 20:6–7

*D*o not fear for the youth and for your maidservant. All that Sarah says to you, listen to her voice, because through Isaac will your descendants be called. However, I will also make the son of the maidservant into a nation, because he is of your seed.

Genesis 21:12–13

What troubles you, Hagar? Do not fear, for God has heard the voice of the youth, as he is there. Arise, lift up the youth and hold him tightly in your hands, for I will make him into a great nation.

Genesis 21:17–18

Abraham!

Genesis 22:1

Now take your son, your only one, whom you love, Isaac, and go for yourself to the land of Moriah. Then, bring him up there as an ascension-offering on one of the mountains of which I will tell you.

Genesis 22:2

Abraham, Abraham!

Genesis 22:11

Do not stretch your hand toward the youth and do not do anything to him, because now I know that you fear God. Therefore you have not withheld your son, your only one, from me.

Genesis 22:12

I have sworn to myself, says the Eternal, that because you did this thing and did not withhold your son, your only one, therefore I will indeed bless you and multiply your descendants as the stars of heaven and as the sand which is on the shore of the sea. Your descendants will inherit the gate of their enemies, and all the nations of the world will be blessed by your descendants, because you listened to me.

Genesis 22:16–18

*T*wo nations are in your womb, and two races will separate from your bowels; and one nation will be stronger than the other nation, and the greater will serve the younger.

Genesis 25:23

*D*o not go down to Egypt. Dwell in the land of which I will tell you. Live in this land, and I will be with you and bless you, because I will give all these lands to you and to your descendants. I will uphold the oath which I swore to Abraham, your father. I will multiply your descendants as the stars of heaven. I will give all these lands to your descendants. All the nations of the earth will be blessed by your descendants, because Abraham listened to me and safeguarded my observance, my commandments, my decrees, and my laws.

Genesis 26:2–5

I am the God of Abraham your father. Fear not, for I am with you. I will bless you, and I will multiply your descendants for the sake of Abraham my servant.

Genesis 26:24

I am the Eternal, God of Abraham your father, and God of Isaac. I will give the land upon which you are lying to you and to your descendants, and your descendants will be as the dust of the earth. Then you will spread westward, eastward, northward, and southward, and all the families of the land will be blessed by you and by your descendants. Now then, I am with you and will safeguard you everywhere you go. I will return you to this land, because I will not abandon you until I have done that which I have spoken to you.

Genesis 28:13–15

◊ ◊ ◊

*R*eturn to the land of your fathers and to your birthplace. I will be with you.

Genesis 31:3

*B*e on guard, yourself, that you do not speak with Jacob for good or for evil.

Genesis 31:24

◇　◇　◇

*S*end me away, because the dawn has risen.

Genesis 32:26

◇　◇　◇

*W*hat is your name?

Genesis 32:27

◇　◇　◇

*Y*our name will no longer be Jacob but Israel, because you have struggled with God and with men and have prevailed.

Genesis 32:28

◇　◇　◇

*W*hy do you ask my name?

Genesis 32:29

◇　◇　◇

*A*rise, go up to Beth-el, and live there. Make there an altar to God who appeared to you when you fled from Esau your brother.

Genesis 35:1

◇　◇　◇

*Y*our name is Jacob. Your name will no longer be Jacob, but Israel will be your name.

Genesis 35:10

◇　◇　◇

I am God Almighty. Be fruitful and multiply. A nation and an assembly of nations will come from you, and kings will come out of your loins; and the land which I gave to Abraham and to Isaac, I will give to you. I will give the land to your descendants after you.

Genesis 35:11–12

*J*acob, Jacob!

Genesis 46:2

◇   ◇   ◇

I am the God, God of your father. Do not fear going down to Egypt, because, there I will make you into a great nation. I will descend with you to Egypt, and I will raise you up again. And Joseph will set his hands on your eyes.

Genesis 46:3–4

EXODUS

Moses, Moses!

Exodus 3:4

◇　◇　◇

Do not approach here. Remove your shoes from your feet, for the place on which you are standing is holy ground.

Exodus 3:5

◇　◇　◇

I am the God of your father, God of Abraham, God of Isaac, and God of Jacob.

Exodus 3:6

◇　◇　◇

I have surely seen the suffering of my people who are in Egypt and have heard their cries in the face of their oppressors, so I know of their sorrows. Therefore, I have descended to rescue them from the hand of Egypt and to raise them from that land to a good and broad land, to a land flowing with milk and honey, to the place of the Canaanite, the Hittite, the Amorite, the Perizzite, the Hivite, and the Jebusite. Even now, here, the cry of the children of Israel comes to me. Moreover, I have seen the affliction with which the Egyptians afflict them. Therefore, go now, and I will send you to Pharaoh, so you may bring my people, the children of Israel, out of Egypt.

Exodus 3:7–10

◇   ◇   ◇

*B*ecause I will be with you. And this is the sign for you that I have sent you: when you bring the people out of Egypt, you will serve God on this mountain.

Exodus 3:12

◇   ◇   ◇

I Am Who I Am! Say thus to the children of Israel: I Am sent me to you.

Exodus 3:14

◇   ◇   ◇

*S*ay thus to the children of Israel: The Eternal, the God of your fathers, God of Abraham, God of Isaac, and God of Jacob, has sent me to you. This is my name forever, and this is my remembrance from generation to generation.

Exodus 3:15

◇   ◇   ◇

*G*o and gather the elders of Israel and say to them: The Eternal, the God of your fathers, God of Abraham, Isaac, and Jacob, appeared to me, saying: I have taken account of you and of what was done to you in Egypt. Therefore, I have said: I will bring you up from the affliction of Egypt to the land of the Canaanite, the Hittite, the Amorite, the Perizzite, the Hivite, and the Jebusite, to a land flowing with milk and honey. Then they will heed you. You will come, you and the elders of Israel, to the King of Egypt and say go him: The Eternal, God of the Hebrews, has called on us, and now, please let us go three days' journey into the desert, so we may sacrifice to the Eternal, our God! But I know that the King of Egypt will not let you go, unless by a strong hand, so I will stretch my hand and strike the Egyptians with all my wonders which I will make among them. And afterwards, he will deliver you. Also, I will give this people favor in the eyes of the Egyptians, so that when you go, you will not go empty-handed. Therefore, each woman will ask her neighbor and her house-boarder for vessels of silver, vessels of gold and gowns. You will put them on your sons and on your daughters and will despoil the Egyptians.

Exodus 3:16–22

*W*hat is this in your hand?

Exodus 4:2

*T*hrow it to the ground.

Exodus 4:3

*E*xtend your hand and grasp its tail.

Exodus 4:4

*I*n order that they believe the Eternal, God of your fathers, God of Abraham, God of Isaac, and God of Jacob appeared to you: bring your hand to your chest.

Exodus 4:5–6

*R*eturn your hand to your chest.

Exodus 4:7

*I*t will be, if they do not believe you and are not convinced by the first sign, that they may be convinced by the latter sign. And it will be, if also they do not believe these two signs and do not listen to your voice, then you will take from the waters of the river and pour them on the land. And the water which you take from the river will become blood on the land.

Exodus 4:8–9

*W*ho has made a mouth for man, and who makes the mute, the deaf, the seeing, or the blind: is it not I, the Eternal? So go, now, and I will be with your mouth and will instruct you what to say.

Exodus 4:11–12

*I*s not Aaron the Levite your brother? I know that he must surely speak. And also now, he is going out to greet you; and when he sees you, he will be glad in his heart. You will speak to him and put the words in his mouth. And I will be with your mouth and with his mouth, and I will instruct you what to do. He will speak to the people for you and be as a mouth for you, and you will be his superior. And take this staff in your hand, with which you will do the signs.

Exodus 4:14–17

*G*o! Return to Egypt, for all the men who sought your life have died.

Exodus 4:19

◇   ◇   ◇

*W*hen you go back to Egypt, let all the wonders that I have put in your hand be seen, and do them before Pharaoh. I will strengthen his heart, and he will not deliver the people. Therefore, you will say to Pharaoh: So says the Eternal: Israel is my firstborn. And I say to you: Deliver my son so he may serve me! And if you refuse to deliver him, then I will kill your son, your firstborn.

Exodus 4:21–23

◇   ◇   ◇

*G*o meet Moses in the desert.

Exodus 4:27

◇   ◇   ◇

*N*ow you will see what I will do to Pharaoh, because he will send them away with a strong hand. And with a strong hand, he will expel them from his land.

Exodus 6:1

I am the Eternal. I appeared to Abraham, to Isaac, and to Jacob as God Almighty, but I was not known to them by my name: the Eternal. And also, I established my contract with them—to give them the land of Canaan, the land of their dwelling, in which they have dwelled. And also, I have heard the groaning of the children of Israel whom Egypt enslaves and have remembered my contract. Therefore, say to the children of Israel: I am the Eternal. I will bring you out from under the burdens of Egypt. I will rescue you from their enslavement. I will redeem you with an outstretched arm and with great judgments. I will take you to me as a people. I will be God to you. You will know that I am the Eternal your God who brought you out from under the burdens of Egypt. I will bring you to the land which I swore to give to Abraham, to Isaac, and to Jacob. I will give it to you as an inheritance. I am the Eternal.

Exodus 6:2–8

*C*ome, speak to Pharaoh, King of Egypt, that he deliver the children of Israel from his land.

Exodus 6:11

I am the Eternal. Tell Pharaoh, King of Egypt, all that I tell you.

Exodus 6:29

◇   ◇   ◇

*S*ee, I have made you as a superior to Pharaoh. And Aaron, your brother, will be your prophet. You will say all that I have commanded you; and Aaron, your brother, will speak to Pharaoh, that he deliver the children of Israel from his land. But I will harden Pharaoh's heart and multiply my signs and wonders in the land of Egypt. And Pharaoh will not listen to you. Therefore, I will put my hand over Egypt and bring out my armies, my people, the children of Israel, from the land of Egypt with great judgments. And when I stretch out my hand over Egypt and bring out the children of Israel from among them, the Egyptians will know that I am the Eternal.

Exodus 7:1–5

◇   ◇   ◇

*W*hen Pharaoh speaks to you, saying: Prove yourselves—then say to Aaron: Take your staff and throw it in front of Pharaoh. It will become a serpent.

Exodus 7:9

*P*haraoh's heart is heavy. He refuses to deliver the people. Go to Pharaoh in the morning when he goes out to the water, and station yourself to call on him by the bank of the river. Hold the staff that turned into a snake. Say to him: The Eternal, God of the Hebrews, sent me to you, saying: Deliver my people so they may serve me in the desert! Yet, until now, you did not listen. So says the Eternal: By this you will know that I am the Eternal. Here, I will strike with the staff which is in my hand on the water which is in the river, and it will turn into blood. The fish that are in the river will die, the river will stink, and Egypt will languish to drink water from the river.

Exodus 7:14–18

◇   ◇   ◇

*S*ay to Aaron: Take your staff and extend your hand over the waters of Egypt: over their rivers, over their canals, over their ponds, and over every wooden and stone pool of their waters, that they become blood. Then there will be blood in all the land of Egypt.

Exodus 7:19

◇   ◇   ◇

*C*ome to Pharaoh and say to him: So says the Eternal: Deliver my people so they may serve me! But if you refuse to deliver them, I will plague all your borders with frogs. The river will swarm with frogs. They will rise up and enter your houses, your bedrooms, your beds, your servants' houses, your people, your ovens, and your kneading troughs. The frogs will assail you, your people, and all your servants.

Exodus 7:26–29

◇   ◇   ◇

*S*ay to Aaron: Extend your hand with your staff over the rivers, over the canals, and over the ponds, and raise the frogs over the land of Egypt.

Exodus 8:1

*S*ay to Aaron: Extend your staff and strike the dust of the land. There will be lice in all the land of Egypt.

Exodus 8:12

*R*ise early in the morning, station yourself before Pharaoh when he goes out to the water, and say to him: So says the Eternal: Deliver my people so they may serve me! Because, if you do not deliver my people, I will send predators on you, on your servants, on your people, and into your houses. Therefore, on that day the houses of Egypt and also the ground on which they are will be full of predators, in order for you to know that I, the Eternal, am near the earth. I will separate the land of Goshen, on which my people stand, so that no predators will be there. I will put a division between my people and your people. As of tomorrow, this will be the sign.

Exodus 8:16–19

*C*ome to Pharaoh and say to him: So says the Eternal, the God of the Hebrews: Deliver my people so they may serve me! Because, if you refuse to deliver and continue to hold them, then the hand of the Eternal will be on your cattle which are in the field, on the horses, on the donkeys, on the camels, on the bulls, and on the sheep—a very heavy pestilence. The Eternal will distinguish between the cattle of Israel and the cattle of Egypt, and among all of the children of Israel, not a thing will die.

Exodus 9:1–4

*T*omorrow the Eternal will do this thing in the land.

Exodus 9:5

◇ ◇ ◇

*G*et yourselves handfuls of soot from a furnace, and let Moses throw them heavenwards at the eyes of Pharaoh. There will be dust over all the land of Egypt. There will be boil-erupting blisters on man and on beast in all the land of Egypt.

Exodus 9:8–9

◇ ◇ ◇

*R*ise early in the morning and station yourself before Pharaoh. Say to him: So says the Eternal, God of the Hebrews: Deliver my people so they may serve me! Because this time, I will send all my plagues to your heart, and on your servants, and on your people, in order for you to know that there is none like me throughout the earth. For now, had I sent my hand for you and your people to be in the pestilence, you would have disappeared from the earth. But, for this sake have I let you stand: for the sake of your seeing my strength, and in order for my name to be declared throughout the earth. Do you continue to be arrogant to my people so as not to deliver them? Now, at this time tomorrow, I will make rain a hail so heavy that there has been nothing like it in Egypt from the day of its foundation until now. So now, gather together your cattle and all that is yours in the field. On every man and beast found in the field, that is not gathered into the house, the hail will come down and they will die.

Exodus 9:13–19

*E*xtend your hand heavenwards. There will be hail throughout the land of Egypt—on man, on beast, and on every herb of the field in the land of Egypt.

Exodus 9:22

*C*ome to Pharaoh, for I have made his heart and his servants' hearts heavy, so that I may set these, my signs, among them, and so that you may tell in the ears of your son and your son's son how I humiliated the Egyptians, and the signs which I made among them. You will know that I am the Eternal.

Exodus 10:1–2

◇   ◇   ◇

*E*xtend your hand over the land of Egypt—for locusts. They will rise up over the land of Egypt to eat all the herbs of the field, everything that remains from the hail.

Exodus 10:12

◇   ◇   ◇

*E*xtend your hand heavenwards. There will be darkness over the land of Egypt, a darkness which may be felt.

Exodus 10:21

I will bring one more plague on Pharaoh and on Egypt, after which he will deliver you from here. When he delivers you, he will surely drive you out from here. Speak now in the ears of the people, that every man ask from his acquaintance and every woman from her acquaintance—vessels of silver and vessels of gold.

Exodus 11:1–2

*P*haraoh will not heed you; therefore my wonders will be multiplied in the land of Egypt.

Exodus 11:9

*F*or you, this month is the beginning of months. For you, it is the first of the months of the year.

Exodus 12:2

*S*peak to all of the congregation of Israel, saying: On the tenth of this month they are to get themselves, each man, a lamb to a family, a lamb to a household. But if the household is too few for a lamb, then he and the closest neighbor to his house are to take it according to the number of beings. You are to allocate the lamb to each man, as he eats—an unblemished, male, year-old lamb is to be for you. You are to take it from among the sheep or from among the goats. It is to be in your guardianship until the fourteenth day of this month. The entire assembly of the congregation of Israel is to slaughter it at twilight. They are to take from the blood and put it on two doorposts and on the lintel of the houses in which they will eat it. They are to eat the meat on this night. They are to eat it roasted in fire, with unleavened bread and bitter herbs. Do not eat from it raw or boiled in water but roast with fire, its head with its legs and its innards. Also, you are not to let it be left-over until morning. What is left-over from it until morning, you are to burn in fire. And you are to eat it so: your loins girded, your shoes on your feet, your sticks in your hands. You are to eat it in haste. It is a Passover to the Eternal. I will pass through the land of Egypt on this night, and I will strike every firstborn in the land of Egypt, from man until beast. And I will make judgments against all the gods of Egypt. I am the Eternal. The blood on the houses will be a sign for you that you are there. I will see the blood and pass over you, so a plague of slaughter will not befall you as I strike in the land of Egypt. This day will be a memorial to you. You will celebrate it as a holiday to the Eternal. You will celebrate it for generations as an everlasting decree. You are to eat unleavened bread for seven days. Even on the first day, you are to have removed leaven from your houses, because everyone who eats leavened bread from the first day through the seventh day, his soul will be cut off from Israel. Also, there is to be a holy calling for you on the first day and a holy calling on the seventh day. No work may be done on them; but that which may be eaten by every being, that alone may be prepared for you. You are the guard the unleavened bread, because on this very day, I brought your armies out from the land of Egypt. You are to safeguard this day for generations as an everlasting decree. In the first month, on the fourteenth day, in the evening, you are to eat unleavened bread—until the twenty-first day of the month, in the evening. For seven days, leaven is not to be found in your houses, because all who eat leavening, either a foreigner or a native of the land, his soul will be cut off from the congregation of Israel. Do not eat anything leavened. You are to eat unleavened bread in all your dwellings.

Exodus 12:3–20

◇　　◇　　◇

This is the decree of the Passover sacrifice: no heathen may eat from it, but every man's money-bought servant, when you circumcise him, then he may eat from it. An alien and a hired servant may not eat from it. In one house it should be eaten. You may not take the meat outside of the house, and you may not break a bone of it. The entire congregation of Israel is to prepare it, so if a foreigner lives with you, and he would prepare the Passover sacrifice for the Eternal, let every male be circumcised, and then he may approach to prepare it. He is to be as a native of the land. Anyone uncircumcised may not eat from it. There is to be one law for the native and for the foreigner who lives among you.

Exodus 12:43–49

Sanctify every firstborn for me. A firstling of any womb of the children of Israel, man or beast, is mine.

Exodus 13:2

*P*erhaps the people will reconsider when they see war and will return to Egypt?

Exodus 13:17

*T*ell the children of Israel to return and camp before Pi–Hachiroth, between Migdol and the sea. You are to camp by the sea, before Baal–Zephon, opposite it. Pharaoh will say of the children of Israel: They are trapped in the land. The desert has closed in on them. I will strengthen Pharaoh's heart, and he will chase after them. I will be esteemed by Pharaoh and by all his soldiers. Egypt will know that I am the Eternal.

Exodus 14:2–4

*W*hy do you cry out to me? Speak to the children of Israel, that they journey on. And you, raise your staff and extend your hand over the sea, and divide it, so the children of Israel will come through the sea on dry ground. Now then, I will harden the heart of the Egyptians, and they will follow you. I will be esteemed by Pharaoh and by all his soldiers, by his chariots, and by his horsemen. Egypt will know that I am the Eternal when I am esteemed by Pharaoh, by his chariots, and by his horsemen.

Exodus 14:15–18

*E*xtend your hand over the sea, and the waters will return over the Egyptians, over their chariots, and over their horsemen.

Exodus 14:26

*I*f you listen to the voice of the Eternal, your God, and do what is right in his eyes, and heed his commandments, and safeguard all his decrees, I will not put any of the diseases which I have put in Egypt on you, for I am the Eternal, your healer.

Exodus 15:26

*N*ow, I will rain bread from the heavens for you, and the people will go out to gather a daily amount, each day, so that I may test them, whether they will walk in my law or not. On the sixth day, when they prepare what they bring, it should be double what they gather daily.

Exodus 16:4–5

I have heard the complaints of the children of Israel. Speak to them, saying: At twilight, you are to eat meat, and in the morning, you will be satisfied with bread. You will know that I am the Eternal, your God.

Exodus 16:12

*H*ow long will you refuse to safeguard my commandments and my law? See, because the Eternal gives you the Sabbath, therefore he gives you bread on the sixth day for two days. Everyone is to stay in his place. No one may leave his place on the seventh day.

Exodus 16:28–29

*P*ass before the people and take with you of the elders of Israel. Hold your staff with which you struck the river and go. Behold, I will stand before you on the rock at Horeb. Strike the rock. Water will come forth, and the people will drink.

Exodus 17:5–6

*W*rite this as a memorial in the book, and put it in Joshua's ears, because I must wipe out the remembrance of Amalek from under the heavens.

Exodus 17:14

◇   ◇   ◇

*S*ay this to the house of Jacob, and tell the children of Israel: You have seen what I have done to the Egyptians, how I lifted you up on the wings of eagles and brought you to me. Now then, if you heed me and safeguard my contract, you will be the treasure of all the nations to me, for the whole earth is mine. You will be to me a kingdom of priests and a holy nation. These are the words you are to speak to the children of Israel.

Exodus 19:3–6

*N*ow, I come to you in a thick cloud so the people will hear when I speak with you and also believe in you forever.

Exodus 19:9

*G*o to the people and prepare them today and tomorrow. They are to wash their clothes, so they will be ready for the third day, because on the third day, the Eternal will descend on Mount Sinai, before the eyes of the all the people. Also, you are to make a boundary around the people, saying: Guard yourselves from ascending the mountain or touching its border. Anyone who touches the mountain must die. Not a hand may touch it, but he must be thrown down and stoned. Whether beast or man, he will not live. During the horn-blast, they may ascend the mountain.

Exodus 19:10–13

*D*escend! Warn the people not to break through to see the Eternal or many of them will fall. And also, the priests who approach the Eternal must sanctify themselves, or the Eternal will erupt in their midst.

Exodus 19:21–22

*G*o! Get down! Then you may ascend with Aaron. But the priests and the people may not break through to ascend towards the Eternal or he will erupt in their midst.

Exodus 19:24

I am the Eternal, your God, who brought you out from the land of Egypt, from the house of slaves. You may have no other gods before me. Do not make yourselves an idol of any image which is in the heavens above, in the earth below, or in the waters beneath the earth. Do not bow to them and do not serve them. For I, the Eternal, your God, am a jealous God, avenging the sin of the fathers on their children, until the third and until the fourth generations of my opponents, and making grace for a thousand generations for my devotees and for the guardians of my commandments. Do not take the name of the Eternal, your God, in vain, for the Eternal will not acquit anyone who takes his name in vain. Remember the Sabbath day, to sanctify it. You may labor six days and do all your work, but the seventh day is a Sabbath to the Eternal your God. You will do no work: you, your son, your daughter, your servant, your maid, your beast, or the stranger within your gates, because in six days the Eternal made the heavens and the earth, the sea and all that is in them, and he rested on the seventh day. Therefore the Eternal blessed the Sabbath day and sanctified it. Honor your father and mother, so your days may be lengthened on the earth which the Eternal, your God, has given to you. Do not murder. Do not commit adultery. Do not steal. Do not testify against your neighbor as a false witness. Do not desire your neighbor's house. Do not desire your neighbor's wife, his servant, his maid, his ox, his donkey, or anything belonging to your neighbor.

Exodus 20:2–14

◇　◇　◇

Say thus to the children of Israel: You have seen that I have spoken with you from the heavens. Do not make any representation of me. Do not make gods of silver or gods of gold for yourselves. Make an altar of earth for me, and sacrifice your ascension-offering and your peace-offering on it—your sheep and your bull. I will come to you and bless you in every place where my name is remembered. And when you make me an altar of stone, do not build it with cut stone. If you wield your sword over it, it is desecrated. Also, do not ascend by stairs onto my altar, so that you do not expose your nakedness upon it.

Exodus 20:19–23

And these are judgments that you are to put before them: If you buy a Hebrew servant, he is to serve six years, and then he will go free in the seventh, gratuitously. If he came alone, he will go alone. If he is a husband, his wife will go with him. If his master has given him a woman, and she has borne him sons and daughters, the woman and her children will be her master's, and he will go out alone. But if the servant says: "I love my master, my woman, and my children. I will not go free," his master is to bring him to the judges and bring him to the door or to the doorpost. His master is to pierce his ear with an awl, and he will serve him forever. Also, if a man sells his daughter as a maid, she is not to go out as the servants go out. If she is evil in the eyes of her master, who was to know her, she must be released. He has no right to sell her to a foreign people, having deceived her. And if she is to be known to his son, he must grant her the rights of a daughter. If he takes another for himself, he may not reduce her dowry, her wardrobe, or her conjugal rights. But if he does not do these three for her, she will go free gratuitously.

Exodus 21:1–11

◇   ◇   ◇

*H*e who strikes a man, so he dies, must die. And for him who did not premeditate, but God has brought it to his hands, I will appoint a place for you where he may flee. And if a man contrives against his neighbor, to kill him intentionally, you may even take him away from my altar to die. And he who strikes his father or his mother must die. And he who kidnaps a man and sells him, and he (the victim) is found in his hand, must die. He who curses his father or his mother must die. Also, if men quarrel, and a man strikes his neighbor with a stone or with his fist, and he does not die but falls bedridden: if he gets up and goes out on his own support, then he who struck is innocent, but he (the aggressor) must give compensation until he (the victim) is completely healed. And if a man strikes his servant or his maid with a stick, and he dies by his hand, he must be avenged. However, if he stands for a day or two, he may not be avenged, because he is his money. And if men fight and hurt a pregnant woman and her child is still-born, yet there be no calamity, he must be fined according to what the husband imposes on him and is granted in court. But if there be a calamity, you are to give a soul for a soul, an eye for eye, a tooth for a tooth, a hand for a hand, a leg for a leg, a burn for a burn, a wound for a wound, a welt for a welt. Therefore, if a man strikes the eye of his servant or the eye of his maid so it is destroyed, he will set him free on account of his eye. And if the tooth of his servant or the tooth of his maid has fallen out, he is to set him free on account of his tooth.

Exodus 21:12–27

And if an ox gores a man or a woman, so he dies, the ox must be stoned, but its meat may not be eaten; yet the owner of the ox is innocent. However, if this ox gored also yesterday and two days ago, and its owner was warned but did not guard it, and it kills a man or a woman, the ox is to be stoned, and also its owner is to die. If a fine is imposed on him, he is to give all that is imposed on him for the redemption of his soul. Whether it gored a son or gored a daughter, it will be done to him according to this judgment. If the ox gores a servant or a maid, he is to give thirty silver shekels to his master, and the ox is to be stoned.

Exodus 21:28–32

And if a man opens a pit, or if a man digs a pit and does not cover it, and an ox or a donkey falls there, the owner of the pit is to pay. He is to return money to its owner, and the carcass will be his (the original owner's). And if a man's ox hurts his neighbor's ox so it dies, they are to sell the living ox and split the money, and they are also to split the carcass. Or, if it is known that this ox gored yesterday and two days ago, and its owner did not guard it, he must pay an ox for an ox, and the carcass will be his (the original owner's). If a man steals an ox or a lamb and slaughters it or sells it, he will pay five bulls for the ox and four sheep for the lamb.

Exodus 21:33:37

If the thief is found breaking in and is struck and dies, there is no liability for him. But if the sun shines on him (he does it in plain view and is not aggressive), there is liability for him. He must pay. If he does not have (enough money to pay), then he may be sold for his theft. If the booty is found alive in his hands, be it an ox, a donkey, or a lamb, he is to pay double.

Exodus 22:1–3

If a man ruins a field or a vineyard by sending cattle to graze in another's field, he is to pay from the best of his field and from the best of his vineyard. If a fire spreads and catches thornbrush and consumes corn stacks or corn stalks, the igniter of the conflagration must pay. If a man gives his neighbor money or utensils to guard, and it is stolen from the man's house: If the thief is found, he is to pay double. If the thief is not found and if he (the guardian) did not send his hand into the property of his neighbor, the owner of the house should approach the judges. For any unjust word about an ox, a donkey, a lamb, a garment, or about any lost thing which he says is his, the word of both of them (the two neighbors) is to come before the judges. Whomever the judges condemn is to pay double to his neighbor. If a man gives his neighbor a donkey, an ox, a lamb, or any beast to guard, and it dies, is hurt, or is snatched without being seen, an oath of the Eternal will be taken between the two of them. If he did not send his hand into the property of his neighbor, its owner is to accept it (his neighbor's word), and he is not to pay. But if it was stolen from him, he is to pay its owner. If it is torn, he should bring him a witness of it. He is not to pay for the torn. Also, if a man borrows from his neighbor, and it is hurt or dies, its owner not being with it, he (the borrower) must pay. If its owner is with it, he is not to pay. If it was rented, it came for its rent.

Exodus 22:4–14

And if a man tempts a virgin who is not engaged and lies with her, he must quickly acquire her as a wife. If her father refuses to give her to him, he (the seducer) is to weigh out money according to the price of virgins.

Exodus 22:15–16

A witch may not live. Whoever lies with a beast must die.

Exodus 22:17–18

He who sacrifices to gods besides the Eternal alone will be annihilated.

Exodus 22:19

Do not cheat, and do not oppress a foreigner, for you were foreigners in the land of Egypt. Do not afflict any widow or orphan. If you afflict him so he cries out to me, I will heed his cry. My anger will rage, and I will kill you with a sword. Your wives will become widows and your children, orphans.

Exodus 22:20–23

*I*f you lend money to my people, to the poor among you, do not be as a creditor to him. Do not lay interest on him. If you put a lien on your neighbor's garment, return it to him by sunset. For it is his only covering. It is his dress for his skin. In what will he lie? It will be, if he calls to me, I will heed, because I am gracious.

Exodus 22:24–26

*D*o not curse judges, and do not curse leaders of your people. Do not delay from your abundance and vintage. You are to give me the firstborn of your sons. You are to do so to your oxen, to your sheep. It will be with its mother seven days. On the eighth day, you are to give it to me. You are to be holy men to me. Also, do not eat meat torn in the field. Throw it to the dogs.

Exodus 22:27–30

*D*o not endure a false hearing. Do not raise your hand with the guilty to be an unjust witness. Do not follow majorities to evil, and do not testify in a dispute and be swayed by majorities. Also, do not favor the meek in his dispute.

Exodus 23:1–3

$\diamond \quad \diamond \quad \diamond$

*I*f you meet your enemy's ox or his donkey wandering, you must return it to him. If you see your enemy's donkey collapsing under its burden, can you abstain from helping him? You must help him.

Exodus 23:4–5

$\diamond \quad \diamond \quad \diamond$

*D*o not pervert the justice of your needy in his dispute. Keep far from a false word, and do not execute the innocent and the acquitted, for I will not acquit the guilty. Do not take a bribe, for the bribe blinds the prudent and perverts the words of the righteous. Do not oppress a foreigner, for you know the soul of the foreigner, because you were foreigners in the land of Egypt.

Exodus 23:6–9

*Y*ou are to sow your land for six years and gather its produce. But in the seventh, you are to leave it idle and abandoned so that the needy of your people may eat, and the animals of the field may eat the leftovers. Likewise you are to do with your vineyard and your olive grove. For six days, you are to do your work, and on the seventh day, you are to make a Sabbath, so your ox and your donkey may rest, and the son of your maid and the foreigner may be refreshed. Safeguard all that I have said to you, and do not mention the name of other gods. It is not to be heard from your mouth.

Exodus 23:10–13

◇ ◇ ◇

*Y*ou are to celebrate three pilgrimages a year for me: You are to keep the festival of unleavened bread. Seven days you are to eat unleavened bread as I have commanded you, in the season of the month of Spring, because in it you left Egypt. And do not appear before me empty-handed. And the festival of the harvest of the first-fruits of your produce, which you have sown in the field. And the festival of the ingathering, at the end of the year, when you have gathered in your produce from the field. Three times a year all your males are to appear before the Lord, the Eternal. Do not sacrifice the blood of my sacrifice with leavened bread. The fat of my festival is not to remain until morning. You will bring the best of the first-fruits of your land to the house of the Eternal your God.

Exodus 23:14–19

◇ ◇ ◇

*D*o not boil a kid in its mother's milk.

Exodus 23:19

◇ ◇ ◇

*B*ehold, I send a messenger before you to guard you on the way and to bring you to the place which I have prepared. Be on guard before him and listen to his voice. Do not rebel against him, because he will not bear your sins, for my name is within him. Hence, if you will listen to his voice and do all that I say, I will be an enemy of your enemies and an opponent of your opponents. For my messenger will go before you and bring you against the Amorite, the Hittite, the Perizzite, the Canaanite, the Hivite, and the Jebusite, and I will destroy them. Do not bow to their gods. Do not serve them. Do not do as they do, for you must demolish them and smash their statues. You are to serve the Eternal your God, that your bread and water be blessed, and I will remove disease from among you. There will not be a bereaved or barren woman in your land. I will fulfill the number of your days. I will set my terror before you and confuse all the people whom you will oppose. I will give the neck of all your enemies to you. I will send hornets before you that will drive out the Hivite, the Canaanite, and the Hittite from before you. I will not drive them out from before you in one year, because the land would become desolate, and the animals of the field would multiply against you. Little by little, I will drive them out from before you, until you are fruitful. You will inherit the land. I will establish your borders from the Sea of Suf until the sea of the Philistines, and from the desert until the river, for I will give the inhabitants of the land into your hand. You will drive them out from before you. Do not make a treaty with them or with their gods. They are not to inhabit your land, because they may make you sin against me, for you might serve their gods. It would only be a trap for you.

Exodus 23:20–33

*G*o up to the Eternal, you and Aaron, Nadav and Avihu, and seventy of the elders of Israel, and bow from afar. Moses alone is to approach to the Eternal. They, however, may not approach, and the people may not ascend with him.

Exodus 24:1–2

*A*scend to me, up the mountain, and be there. To you I will give the stone tablets, the law, and the commandments which I have written, to teach them.

Exodus 24:12

*S*peak to the children of Israel, that they take an offering for me. You are to take my offering from every man whose heart will contribute. And this is the offering that you will take from them: gold, silver, copper, blue wool, purple, and scarlet-crimson, linen, angora, reddened ram's skin, lamb skin, acacia wood, oil for the light, spices for the anointing oil and for the incense of spices, onyx stones, and setting stones for the vest and breastplate. They are to make a sanctuary for me, and I will be present among them. According to all that I show you, the plan of the sanctuary and the design of all its utensils, so will you make it.

Exodus 25:1–9

*T*hey are to make an ark of acacia wood. Its length—two and a half forearms; and its width—one and a half forearms; and its height—one and a half forearms. Overlay it with pure gold. Overlay it inside and outside, and make a band of gold around it. Cast four rings of gold for it and put them on its four corners—two rings on its first side and two rings on its second side. Make poles of acacia wood, and overlay them with gold. Bring the poles into the rings on the sides of the ark, to lift the ark on them. The poles will be in the rings of the ark. They may not be removed from them. Place in the ark the testimony which I will give you.

Exodus 25:10–16

*Y*ou are to make a covering of pure gold. Its length—two and a half forearms; its width—one and a half forearms. Make two gold cherubs. Make them beaten out from the two ends of the covering. Make one cherub from this end and one cherub from that end. Make the cherubs from the covering, on its two ends. The cherubs will be spreading their wings upwards, sheltering the covering with their wings, and their faces toward one another. The faces of the cherubs will be towards the covering. Place the covering on the ark from above and put the testimony which I give you into the ark. I will be met by you there and will speak to you from above the covering, from between the two cherubs which are on the ark of the testimony, about all that I command you concerning the children of Israel.

Exodus 25:17–22

*Y*ou are to make a table of acacia wood. Its length—two forearms; its width—one forearm; its height—one and a half forearms. Overlay it with pure gold, and make a band of gold around it. Make a handbreadth frame around it and make a gold band encircling its frame. Make four gold rings for it and put the rings on the four corners which are by its four feet. The rings will be against the frame as housings for the poles to lift the table. Make the poles from acacia wood and overlay them with gold. The table will be carried on them. Make its dishes, its spoons, its supports, and its racks to protect them. Make them of pure gold. Place shew-bread on the table, always before me.

Exodus 25:23–30

◇   ◇   ◇

You are to make a candelabrum of pure gold. The candelabrum is to be made beaten out. Its base, its shaft, its cups, its knobs, and its flowers will be from it. And six branches will extend from its sides—three candelabrum branches from the first side and three candelabrum branches from the second side. Three almond-shaped cups, a knob, and a flower on one branch, and three almond-shaped cups, a knob, and a flower on one branch. Likewise for all six branches which extend from the candelabrum. And on the candelabrum—four almond-shaped cups, its knobs, and its flowers. And a knob under the two branches from it, and a knob under the two branches from it, and a knob under the two branches from it, for the six branches which go out from the candelabrum. Their knobs and their branches are to be from it, all of it beaten out of a unit of pure gold. You are to make its seven lamps. Its lamps are to be raised and are to shine across its face. Also, its tongs and its ash-pans: pure gold. Make all these utensils from a talent of pure gold and observe and produce according to their design which you were shown on the mountain.

Exodus 25:31–40

◇   ◇   ◇

You are to make the tabernacle of ten curtains: woven linen, blue wool, purple, and scarlet-crimson. Make them with meticulously produced cherubs. The length of one curtain—twenty-eight forearms; and the width of one curtain—four forearms: one measurement for all the curtains. Five curtains are to be joined, one to the next, and five curtains joined, one to the next. Make loops of blue wool on the edge of the one curtain at the end of the group, and do so on the edge of the last curtain in the second group. Make fifty loops in the one curtain and fifty loops in the end curtain which is in the second group, the loops being parallel, one to the next. Make fifty golden clasps and join the curtains with the clasps, one to the next. The tabernacle will be one.

Exodus 26:1–6

*Y*ou are to make angora curtains as a tent over the tabernacle. Make eleven curtains. The length of one curtain—thirty forearms; the width of one curtain—four forearms: one measurement for the eleven curtains. Join five curtains apart, and six curtains apart, and fold the sixth curtain opposite the front of the tent. Make fifty loops on the edge of the one last curtain in the group and fifty loops on the edge of the curtain of the second group. Make fifty copper clasps, and join the clasps to the loops, and join the tent, so it will be one. Hang the overhanging excess of the curtains of the tent, the overhanging half of the curtain, over the back of the tabernacle. The length of the curtains of the tent, the forearm from this and the forearm from that, in excess, is to be hung on the sides of the tabernacle, from this and from that, to cover it. Make a covering for the tent of reddened ram's skin and a covering of lamb's skin, above.

Exodus 26:7–14

◇   ◇   ◇

*Y*ou are to make standing boards of acacia wood for the tabernacle. The length of the board—ten forearms; and the width of the one board—a forearm and a half forearm. Two tenons for the one board, interlocked, one to the next. Do likewise for all the boards of the tabernacle. Make the boards for the tabernacle thus: twenty boards for the south side, southwards. Make forty silver sockets under the twenty boards—two sockets under each board for its two tenons and two sockets under each board for its two tenons. And for the second rib of the tabernacle, the north side, twenty boards and their forty silver sockets— two sockets under each board and two sockets under each board. And make six boards for the rear of the tabernacle, westwards. And make two boards for the corners at the rear of the tabernacle. They are to be coupled below and coupled together on top by one ring. Likewise for the two of them. They will be for the two corners. There will be eight boards and their silver sockets, sixteen sockets—two sockets under each board and two sockets under each board.

Exodus 26:15–25

◇   ◇   ◇

*Y*ou are to make latches of acacia wood: five for the boards of the first rib of the tabernacle, and five latches for the second rib of the tabernacle, and five latches for the boards of the rib at the rear of the tabernacle, westwards. However, the middle latch, inside the boards, will latch from end to end. Overlay the boards with gold and make their rings, housing for the latches, of gold. Overlay the latches with gold. Erect the tabernacle in its fashion, as you were shown on the mountain.

Exodus 26:26–30

◇　◇　◇

You are to make a veil of blue wool, purple, scarlet-crimson and woven linen. Make it with meticulously produced cherubs. Place it on four acacia posts overlaid with gold, and their hooks of gold, in four silver sockets. Place the veil under the clasps and bring the ark of the testimony there, within the veil. The veil will be a division for you between the holy and the Holiest of Holies. You are to place the covering on the ark of the testimony in the Holiest of Holies. You are to put the table outside the veil and the candelabrum opposite the table, by the southern rib of the tabernacle. Place the table by the north rib. Make a screen for the entrance of the tent of blue wool, purple, scarlet-crimson and woven linen, the work of an embroiderer. Make five acacia posts for the screen, and overlay them with gold; and their hooks, of gold. Cast five sockets of copper for them.

Exodus 26:31–37

◇　◇　◇

You are to make an altar of acacia wood, five forearms long and five forearms wide. The altar will be square, and its height—three forearms. Make its horns on its four corners. Its horns will be of it. Overlay it with copper. Make its fire-pots, its shovels, its basins, its forks, and its ash-pans. Make all of its utensils of copper. Make a copper network grating for it, and put four copper rings on the net, on its four ends. Place it under the rim of the altar, below, so the net will be in the middle of the altar. Make poles for the altar, poles of acacia wood, and overlay them with copper. The poles will be put into the rings, and the poles will be on the two ribs of the altar, for lifting it. Make it of hollow planks. As it was shown to you on the mountain, so they will make it.

Exodus 27:1–8

◇　◇　◇

You are to make the enclosure of the tabernacle. For the south side of the enclosure, southwards—hangings of woven linen, a hundred forearms long for each side. And its posts—twenty. And their sockets—twenty of copper. The hooks of the posts and their fasteners—silver. And so for the length of the north side—hangings, hundred-length. And its posts—twenty. And their sockets—twenty of copper. The hooks of the posts and their fasteners—silver. For the width of the enclosure along the west side—hangings, fifty forearms. Their posts—ten; and their sockets—ten. For the width of the enclosure along the front side, eastwards—fifty forearms. Also, fifteen forearms of hangings for the shoulder. Their posts—three; and their sockets—three. And for the second shoulder—fifteen hangings. Their posts—three; and their sockets—three. And for the gate of the enclosure—a screen of twenty forearms of blue wool, purple, scarlet-crimson, and woven linen, the work of an embroiderer. Their posts—four; and their sockets—four. All the posts encircling the enclosure will be fastened with silver. And their hooks—silver; and their sockets—copper. The length of the enclosure—a hundred forearms. And width—fifty in fifty; and height—five forearms of woven linen. And their sockets—of copper. For all the utensils of the tabernacle, in all of its service, and all of its pegs, and all the pegs of the enclosure—copper.

Exodus 27:9–19

◇   ◇   ◇

And you are to command the children of Israel, that they bring you pure, pressed, olive oil for lighting, to raise a lamp continually. Aaron and his sons will tend it from evening until morning in the tent of meeting, outside the veil which is above the testimony, before the Eternal, an everlasting decree for your generations of the children of Israel.

Exodus 27:20–21

◇   ◇   ◇

And you, let Aaron your brother, and his sons with him, approach you from among the children of Israel to be priests for me: Aaron, Nadav and Avihu, Eleazar and Ithamar—Aaron's sons. You are to make holy garments for Aaron your brother, for honor and for glory. Therefore, speak to all the wise-hearted whom I have filled with the spirit of wisdom. They will make Aaron's garments to sanctify him to be a priest for me. These are the garments which they are to make: a breastplate, a vest, a robe, a plaid shirt, a turban, and a belt. They will make holy garments for Aaron your brother and for his sons, to be priests for me. Therefore, they will take the gold, the blue wool, the purple, the scarlet-crimson, and the linen.

Exodus 28:1–5

◆   43   ◆

*T*hey are to make the vest: gold, blue wool, purple, scarlet-crimson, and woven linen, meticulously produced. It will have two joined shoulders at its two ends, also joined. And the girdle of its vest which is on it, like its work, will be of it: gold, blue wool, purple, scarlet-crimson, and woven linen. Take two onyx stones and engrave the names of the children of Israel on them: six of their names on the first stone and the six remaining names on the second stone, according to their birth, the work of a stonecutter, signet-like engravings. Engrave the two stones with the names of the children of Israel. You are to make them encircled with gold settings. Put the two stones on the shoulders of the vest, memorial stones for the children of Israel. Aaron will bear the names before the Eternal, on his two shoulders, as a memorial. Make gold settings and two binding chains of pure gold. Make them of braided work, and put the braided chains on the settings.

Exodus 28:6–14

◇　◇　◇

*Y*ou are to make a breastplate of judgment, meticulously produced. Make it like the work of the vest. Make it of gold, blue wool, purple, scarlet-crimson, and woven linen. It shall be square, folded. Its length—a finger-span; and its width—a finger-span. Set setting stones in it—four rows of stones. The first row: ruby, topaz, emerald—a row. And the second row: turquoise, sapphire, and diamond. And the third row: opal, agate, and amethyst. And the forth row: beryl, onyx, and jasper. They are to be set with gold in their settings, and the stones are to be with with the names of the children of Israel, twelve with their names. Signet-like engravings are to be for the twelve tribes, each with its name. Make binding chains on the breastplate, braided work, pure gold. Make two gold rings on the breastplate, and put the two rings on the two ends of the breastplate. Put the two gold braids on the two rings at the end of the breastplate, and put the two ends of the two braids in the two settings. Put it on the shoulders of the vest, against its front. Make two gold rings, and place them on the two ends of the breastplate, on its border which is opposite the vest, within. Make two gold rings and put them on the two shoulders of the vest, below, against its front, opposite its joints, above the girdle of the vest. Fasten the breastplate by its rings to the rings of the vest with a blue wool cord, to be on the girdle of the vest, so the breastplate does not dislodge from the vest. Aaron is to bear the names of the children of Israel, on the breastplate of judgment, on his heart, when he comes to the sanctuary, as a memorial before the Eternal, continually. Put the Urim and the Thummim on the breastplate of judgment, that they be on Aaron's heart when he comes before the Eternal. Aaron shall bear the judgment of the children of Israel on his heart, before the Eternal, continually.

Exodus 28:15–30

◇　◇　◇

You are to make the robe of the vest entirely of blue wool, and the opening of its head will be in its middle. Its opening is to have an encircling border. It shall have web-work like the opening of chain-mail. It should not be torn. Make, on its hem, pomegranates of blue wool, purple, and scarlet-crimson, on its hem, encircling, and gold bells encircling among them—a gold bell and a pomegranate, a gold bell and a pomegranate, encircling the hems of the robes. It shall be upon Aaron to officiate. His voice will be heard when he enters the sanctuary, before the Eternal, and when he goes out, that he not die.

Exodus 28:31–35

◇　◇　◇

You are to make a headband of pure gold and engrave signet-like engravings on it: Sanctified for the Eternal. Place it on a blue wool string, to be over the turban. It is to be against the front of the turban. It shall be on Aaron's forehead. Aaron shall bear the sin of the sanctifications which the children of Israel will sanctify with all of their sanctified gifts. It is to be on his forehead as goodwill for them, continually before the Eternal. You are to weave the plaid linen shirt, make a linen turban, and make a belt, the work of an embroiderer. Also, make shirts for Aaron's sons, make belts for them, and make hats for them, for honor and for glory. You are to dress them: Aaron your brother and his sons with him. You are to anoint them, consecrate their hands, and sanctify them, so that they be priests for me. Make breechcloths to cover naked flesh. They are to be from the hips to the thighs. They are to be on Aaron and on his sons when they come to the tent of meeting, and when they approach the altar to officiate in the sanctuary, so that they do not bear sin and die—an everlasting decree for him and for his descendants after him.

Exodus 28:36–43

◇　◇　◇

And this is the thing you are to do to them, to sanctify them as priests for me: Take one young bull, two unblemished rams, unleavened bread, unleavened dough mixed in oil, and unleavened wafers anointed in oil—make them of wheat flour—and put them in one basket. Bring them nearby in the basket, also the bull and the two rams. And let Aaron and his sons come close to the entrance of the tent of meeting, so you may bathe them in water. Take the garments and dress Aaron with the shirt, with the robe of the vest, with the vest, and with the breastplate. Vest him in the girdle of the vest. Place the turban on his head and put the holy crown on the turban. Take the anointing oil, pour it on his head, and anoint him. Also, let his sons come close. You are to dress them in shirts, wrap them in belts, Aaron and his sons, and bind hats for them. The priesthood will be for them as an everlasting decree. Consecrate the hands of Aaron and the hands of his sons.

Exodus 29:1–9

◇ ◇ ◇

You are to let the bull come close to the tent of meeting, so Aaron and his sons may lay their hands on the head of the bull. Slaughter the bull before the Eternal by the entrance of the tent of meeting. Take of the blood of the bull and put it on the horns of the altar with your finger, and spill all the blood at the foundation of the altar. Take all the fat that covers the innards, the gland above the liver, the two kidneys and the fat that is on them, and incinerate it on the altar. However, burn the meat of the bull, its skin and its excrement, in fire, outside the camp. It is a sin–offering.

Exodus 29:10–14

◇ ◇ ◇

And you are to take the first ram. Aaron and his sons will lay their hands on the head of the ram. You are to slaughter the ram, take its blood, and sprinkle it around on the altar. Cut the ram into its pieces. Wash its innards and its legs, and put them over its pieces and over its head. Incinerate all of the ram on the altar. It is an ascension–offering to the Eternal, a pleasing aroma. It is a fire–offering to the Eternal.

Exodus 29:15–18

You are to take the second ram. Aaron and his sons will lay their hands on the head of the ram. Slaughter the ram, take of its blood, and put it on the lobe of Aaron's ear and on the lobes of his sons' right ears, on the right thumbs of their hands, and on the right thumbs of their feet. Sprinkle the blood around on the altar. Take of the blood which is on the altar and of the anointing oil, and splash it on Aaron and on his garments, on his sons and on his sons' garments, with him. He and his garments, his sons and his sons' garments, with him, will be sanctified.

Exodus 29:19–21

*Y*ou are to take from the ram: the fat, the rump, the fat that covers the innards, and the gland above the liver, the two kidneys and the fat that is on them, and the right shank—because it is a consecrated ram—and one loaf of bread, one oily dough bread, and one wafer from the basket of unleavened bread which is before the Eternal. Place everything on Aaron's palms and on the palms of his sons, and wave them as a wave–offering before the Eternal. Take them from their hands and incinerate them on the altar with the ascension–offering, as a pleasing aroma before the Eternal. It is a fire–offering to the Eternal.

Exodus 29:22–25

*Y*ou are to take the breast from the consecrated ram which is for Aaron and wave it as a wave–offering before the Eternal. It will be your portion. You are to sanctify the breast of the wave–offering which is to be waved and the shank of the raised–offering which is to be raised, from the consecrated ram—from that of Aaron's and from that of his sons. It is to be for Aaron and for his sons as an everlasting portion from the children of Israel, for it is a raised–offering. Hence, it will be a raised–offering from the children of Israel, from the sacrifices of their peace–offerings, their raised–offering for the Eternal.

Exodus 29:26–28

*A*nd the holy garments which are for Aaron will be for his sons after him, to be anointed in them, and to consecrate their hands in them. The priest succeeding him, from among his sons, who will come into the tent of meeting to officiate in the sanctuary, is to wear them for seven days. Then, you are to take the consecrated ram and cook its meat in a holy place. Aaron and his sons will eat the meat of the ram and the bread which is in the basket, by the entrance of the tent of meeting. They will eat that which has atoned for them, to consecrate their hands, to sanctify them, but the stranger may not eat, for they are holy. Yet, if any of the meat of the consecration or from the bread remains until the morning, burn the remains in fire. Do not eat, for it is holy. You are to do for Aaron and for his sons all that I have commanded you. Consecrate their hands for seven days. Then, prepare a bull, a sin–offering per day, with the atonements. Expiate for the altar with your atonement on it, and anoint it to sanctify it. Atone for the altar for seven days, and sanctify it. The altar is to be the holiest of holies. All that touches the altar will be holy.

Exodus 29:29–37

And this is what you are to prepare on the altar: two one-year-old lambs per day, continually. Prepare the first lamb in the morning, and prepare the second lamb at twilight. And for the first lamb: a tenth of flour mixed in a quarter gallon of beaten oil and a libation of a quarter gallon of wine. And prepare the second lamb at twilight. Prepare it like the morning oblation and like its libation, as a pleasing aroma, a fire–offering to the Eternal, a continual ascension–offering before the Eternal, throughout your generations, by the entrance of the tent of meeting, there, where I will be met by you, to speak to you there. I will be met there by the children of Israel. It is to be sanctified in my honor. I will sanctify the tent of meeting and the altar, and I will sanctify Aaron and his sons to be priests for me. I will be present among the children of Israel and will be their God. They will know that I am the Eternal their God, who brought them out from the land of Egypt to be present among them. I am the Eternal their God.

Exodus 29:38–46

You are to make an altar for burning incense. Make it of acacia wood. Its length—a forearm; its width—a forearm. It will be square. And its height—two forearms; its horns being from it. Overlay it with pure gold: its roof, its surrounding walls, and its horns. Make it an encircling band of gold. And make two gold rings from it, beneath its band, on its two ribs. Make it on its two sides, that they be as housings for the poles, to lift it on them. Make the poles of acacia wood and overlay them with gold. Put it before the veil which is over the ark of the testimony, in front of the covering which is above the testimony, there, where I will be met by you. In the morning, Aaron is to burn incense of spices on it. He is to burn it in the morning when he tends the lamps. When Aaron raises the lamps at twilight, he is to burn it, a perpetual incense before the Eternal, throughout your generations. Do not raise strange incense on it, an ascension–offering, or an oblation, and do not pour a libation over it. Aaron will atone on its horns once a year. He will atone for it once a year with the blood of the sin–offering of atonements, throughout your generations. It is the holiest of holies for the Eternal.

Exodus 30:1–10

◇　◇　◇

When you take the census of the children of Israel by their numbers, each man is to give a ransom for his soul to the Eternal, as you number them. Therefore, there will not be a plague on them while you number them. All who pass with the numbered will give this: half a shekel of the holy shekel, twenty pennyweights per shekel, half the shekel, a raised–offering to the Eternal. All who pass with the numbered, aged twenty years and upwards, will give a raised–offering for the Eternal. The rich may not increase, and the needy may not decrease from the half shekel, to give the raised–offering for the Eternal to atone for your souls. Take the atonement silver from the children of Israel and give it for the service of the tent of meeting. It will be a memorial for the children of Israel, before the Eternal, to atone for your souls.

Exodus 30:12–16

◇　◇　◇

You are to make a copper basin and its copper base for washing. Put it between the tent of meeting and the altar. Put water there. Aaron and his sons are to wash their hands and their feet from it. They are to wash with water when they come to the tent of meeting, or when they approach the altar to officiate, to burn a fire–offering to the Eternal, so they do not die. They will wash their hands and their feet, and they will not die. It is to be an everlasting decree for him and for his descendants, throughout their generations.

Exodus 30:18–21

And you, take fine spices for yourself. Pure myrrh—five hundred; and cinnamon spice, half of it—two hundred and fifty; and calamus spice—two hundred and fifty; and cassia—five hundred in the holy ounce; and olive oil—a gallon. Make it a holy anointing oil, a mixed mixture, the work of a mixer. It is to be a holy anointing oil. You are to anoint with it:

the tent of meeting, the ark of the testimony, the table and all of its utensils, the candelabrum and its utensils, the incense altar, the ascension altar and all of its utensils, and the basin and its base. Sanctify them, so they become the holiest of holies. All that touches them will be sanctified. Then, anoint Aaron and his sons and sanctify them to be priests for me. And speak to the children of Israel, saying: This will be a holy anointing oil for me, throughout your generations. It may not be poured on man's flesh, and do not make any like it, of its composition. It is holy. It will be holy to you. A man who mixes any like it and puts it on a stranger will be cut off from his people.

Exodus 30:23–33

Take spices for yourself: balsam, clove, and galbanum, spices and pure frankincense. It is to be part by part. Make of it an incense, a mixture, the work of a mixer, blended, pure, sanctified. Grind powder from it and put it before the testimony in the tent of meeting, there, where I will be met by you. It will be the holiest of holies for you. Do not prepare the incense which you make, of its composition, for yourselves. It is sanctified to you for the Eternal. A man who produces any like it, to be scented with it, will be cut off from his people.

Exodus 30:34–38

◇   ◇   ◇

See, I have called by name Bezalel son of Uri son of Hur from the tribe of Judah. I have filled him with the spirit of God—in wisdom, in understanding, in knowledge, and in all craft, to devise devices, to work in gold, in silver, in copper, in masoning stone for settings, and in carving wood, to work in every craft. And here, I place with him Aholiab son of Achisamach of the tribe of Dan. Also, I have placed wisdom in the heart of all who are wise-hearted. They will make all that I have commanded you: the tent of meeting, the ark for the testimony and the veil which is over it, all the utensils of the tent, the table and its utensils, the immaculate candelabrum and all of its utensils, the incense altar, the altar of ascension–offering and all of its utensils, the basin and its base, the official garments, the holy garments for Aaron the priest, the garments for his sons to be priests, the anointing oil, and the incense of spices for sanctification. They will do according to all that I have commanded you.

Exodus 31:2–11

*A*nd you, speak to the children of Israel, saying: Surely, you will safeguard my Sabbaths, because it is a sign between me and you, throughout your generations, to know that I, the Eternal, sanctify you. Safeguard the Sabbath, for it is holy to you. The desecrater must die, for whoever does work on it, that soul will be cut off from among its people. You may do work for six days, but on the seventh day—a Sabbath rest, sanctified for the Eternal. Whoever does work on the Sabbath must die. The children of Israel are to safeguard the Sabbath, to make the Sabbath throughout their generations as an everlasting contract. It is a sign between me and the children of Israel, forever, because in six days the Eternal created the heavens and the earth, and on the seventh day he rested and was refreshed.

Exodus 31:13–17

*G*o! Descend, for your people whom you have brought up from the land of Egypt are corrupt. They have deviated quickly from the way which I have commanded them. They have made a molten calf for themselves, have bowed to it, have sanctified to it, and have said: These are your gods, Israel, which have brought you up from the land of Egypt.

Exodus 32:7–8

I have seen this people, and alas, it is a stiff-necked people. Now, therefore, leave it to me. My anger will rage against them. I will devour them and make you into a great nation.

Exodus 32:9–10

I will erase from my book whoever has sinned against me. Now then, go lead the people to the place of which I have spoken to you. Now my messenger will go before you; but on the day of my retribution, I will punish their sins upon them.

Exodus 32:33–34

◇   ◇   ◇

*G*o! Ascend from this, you and the people whom you brought up from the land of Egypt to the land which I promised to Abraham, to Isaac, and to Jacob, saying: I will give it to your descendants. I will send a messenger before you, and I will drive out the Canaanite, the Amorite, the Hittite, the Perizzite, the Hivite, and the Jebusite—to a land flowing with milk and honey. But I will not ascend among you, because you are a stiff-necked people. Perhaps, I would devour you on the way.

Exodus 33:1–3

◇   ◇   ◇

*S*ay to the children of Israel: You are a stiff-necked people. Were I to ascend among you for one minute, I would devour you. Therefore now, cast off your jewelry. I will know what to do with you.

Exodus 33:5

◇   ◇   ◇

*M*y presence will go. I will let you rest.

Exodus 33:14

◇   ◇   ◇

*A*lso, I will do this thing of which you have spoken, because you have found favor in my eyes, and I know you by name.

Exodus 33:17

◇   ◇   ◇

I will pass all my goodness by your face and will call the Eternal before you by name. I will be gracious to whom I will be gracious, and I will be compassionate to whom I will be compassionate.

Exodus 33:19

◇   ◇   ◇

*Y*ou are not able to see my face, because man may not see me and live.

Exodus 33:20

◇   ◇   ◇

*H*ere is a place by me. Station yourself on the rock. When my splendor passes, I will place you in the crevice of the rock, and I will cover my hand over you until I pass. Then, I will remove my hand, and you will see my back, but my face will not be seen.

Exodus 33:21–23

◇ ◇ ◇

Chisel, for yourself, two stone tablets like the first. I will write the words on the tablets which were on the first tablets which you broke. Be prepared in the morning, for in the morning, you will ascend to Mount Sinai and station yourself there, for me, on the top of the mountain. But no man may ascend with you. And also, no man may be seen in all of the mountain. Also, the sheep and the cattle may not graze opposite that mountain.

Exodus 34:1–3

◇ ◇ ◇

The Eternal is the Eternal, God, compassionate, gracious, slow to anger, abundant in mercy and truth, showing mercy to the thousandth generation, bearing iniquity, transgression, and sin, and not destroying the innocent, punishing the iniquity of fathers on their children and on their children's children, until the third and the fourth generations.

Exodus 34:6–7

Now, I am making a contract. I will do wonders before your people, which have not been created in all of the earth or in all of the nations. All the people among whom you are will see the work of the Eternal, because, what I will do with you, it is fearful. Safeguard, for yourself, that which I command you today. Here, I am driving out from before you: the Amorite, the Canaanite, the Hittite, the Perizzite, the Hivite, and the Jebusite. Be on guard, yourself, or you may make a treaty with the inhabitant of the land to which you come. Perhaps he will be a trap in your midst. Therefore, you are to demolish their altars, break their statues, and cut their groves, because you may not bow to another god, because the Eternal, his name is jealous. He is a jealous God. Perhaps you would make a treaty with the inhabitants of the land. They solicit their gods and sacrifice to their gods. He would call on you. You would eat from his sacrifice. You would take from his daughters for your sons. His daughters solicit their gods. Your sons would solicit their gods. Do not make molten gods for yourself.

Exodus 34:10–17

*Y*ou are to safeguard the festival of unleavened bread. You are to eat unleavened bread for seven days as I have commanded you, in the appointed month of Spring, because in the month of Spring, you left Egypt. Every firstling of a womb is mine—hence, all cattle which is a male firstling of an ox or sheep. But you are to redeem a firstling donkey with a sheep; and if you do not redeem it, you are to break its neck. Redeem every firstborn of your sons, and do not appear before me empty-handed. You may work for six days, but you are to rest on the seventh day. Make a Sabbath in plough-time and in harvest, and make the festival of weeks, for yourself, of the first-fruit of the wheat harvest—and the festival of ingathering at its time of the year. Three times a year, all of your males will appear before the Lord, the Eternal, God of Israel, for I will dispossess nations from before you and widen your borders. Yet, no man will desire your land while you ascend to appear before the Eternal three times a year. Do not slaughter the blood of my sacrifice with leaven. And do not leave the Passover festival sacrifice until morning. Bring the best of the first-fruits of your land to the house of the Eternal your God.

Exodus 34:18–26

*D*o not boil a kid in its mother's milk.

Exodus 34:26

*W*rite these words for yourself, because according to these words I have made a contract with you and with Israel.

Exodus 34:27

*Y*ou are to raise the tabernacle of the tent of meeting in a day of the first month, on the first of the month. You are to put the ark of the testimony there and cover the ark with the veil. Bring the table and arrange its arrangements. Bring the candelabrum and raise its lamps. Put the gold altar for incense before the ark of testimony. Place a screen at the entrance to the tabernacle. Put the ascension altar before the entrance of the tabernacle of the tent of meeting. Put the basin between the tent of meeting and the altar, and put water there. Place the enclosure around, and put a screen at the gate of the enclosure. Take the anointing oil and anoint the tabernacle and all which is in it. Sanctify it and all of its utensils, so it will be holy. Anoint the ascension altar and all of its utensils. Sanctify the altar, so the altar will be the holiest of holies. Anoint the basin and its base, and sanctify it. Let Aaron and his sons approach the entrance of the tent of meeting, and bathe them in water. Dress Aaron in the holy garments, anoint him, and sanctify him, so he will be a priest for me. And let his sons approach. You are to dress them in shirts and anoint them as you anointed their father, so they will be priests for me. It will be for them, that their anointing will be as an everlasting priesthood throughout their generations.

Exodus 40:2–15

LEVITICUS

*S*peak to the children of Israel and say to them: When a man among you presents an offering to the Eternal, you are to present your offering from the cattle—from the bulls and from the sheep. If one's offering is an ascension–offering, he is to offer it from the unblemished, male bulls. He is to offer it by the entrance of the tent of meeting, for his acceptance before the Eternal. He is to lay his hand on the head of the ascension–offering so it will be accepted for him, as atonement for him. He is to slaughter the young bull before the Eternal. Aaron's sons, the priests, are to offer the blood and sprinkle the blood around on the altar which is by the entrance of the tent of meeting. He is to skin the ascension–offering and cut it into pieces. The sons of Aaron the priest are to put fire on the altar and arrange wood on the fire. Aaron's sons, the priests, are to arrange the pieces, the head and the fat, on the wood which is on the fire on the altar. He is to wash its innards and its legs in water. The priest will incinerate all of it on the altar as an ascension–offering, a fire–offering, a pleasing aroma for the Eternal.

Leviticus 1:2–9

◇　◇　◇

*A*nd if his offering for the ascension–offering is from the flock, from the sheep or from the goats, he is to offer an unblemished male. He is to slaughter it on the north side of the altar, before the Eternal. Aaron's sons, the priests, will sprinkle the blood around on the altar. He is to cut it into its pieces, with its head and with its fat. The priest will arrange them on the wood which is on the fire on the altar. He is to wash its innards and its legs in water. The priest will offer and incinerate all of it on the altar. It is an ascension–offering, a fire–offering, a pleasing aroma for the Eternal.

Leviticus 1:10–13

And if his offering, an ascension–offering for the Eternal, is from the birds, he is to present his offering from the doves or from the young pigeons. The priest will offer it to the altar, pinch off its head, and incinerate it on the altar. Its blood will be pressed out on the wall of the altar. He is to remove its gizzard from its entrails and fling it beside the altar, eastwards, to the site of the ashes. He is to split it at its wings but not asunder. The priest will incinerate it on the altar, on the wood which is on the fire. It is an ascension–offering, a fire–offering, a pleasing aroma for the Eternal.

Leviticus 1:14–17

And when a person offers a meal–offering for the Eternal, his offering will be flour. He is to pour oil on it and put frankincense on it. He is to bring it to Aaron's sons, the priests. He is to take a handful from there, his full handful, from its flour and from its oil, with all of its frankincense. The priest will incinerate its memorial–portion on the altar, a fire–offering, a pleasing aroma for the Eternal. And the left-over from the meal–offering will be for Aaron and for his sons, the holiest of holies from the fire–offerings of the Eternal.

Leviticus 2:1–3

And when you offer an oven-baked meal–offering, it is to be unleavened doughs of flour mixed in oil and unleavened wafers anointed in oil. If your offering be a meal–offering on the frying-pan, it is to be unleavened flour mixed in oil. Crumble it to crumbs and pour oil on it. It is a meal–offering. And if your offering is a meal–offering from the stir-pot, it is to be made of flour in oil. You are to bring the meal–offering which is made from these for the Eternal. It is to be offered to the priest and brought to the altar. The priest will raise its memorial–portion from the meal–offering and incinerate it on the altar, a fire–offering, a pleasing aroma for the Eternal. And the remainder from the meal–offering will be for Aaron and for his sons, the holiest of holies from the fire–offerings of the Eternal.

Leviticus 2:4–10

*A*ny meal–offering that you offer to the Eternal may not be made of leavening, because you may not incinerate a fire–offering for the Eternal from any leaven or any honey. You may offer them as a first-fruit offering to the Eternal, but they are not to ascend to the altar for a pleasing aroma. Also, you are to season all of your meal–offerings with salt. Hence, you are not to withhold the salt of the covenant of your God from upon your meal–offering. You are to offer all of your offerings with salt. And if you offer a first-fruit meal–offering to the Eternal, you are to offer your first-fruit meal–offering of freshly ground barleycorn roasted in fire. You are to put oil on it and place frankincense on it. It is a meal–offering. The priest will incinerate its memorial–portion from its grind and from its oil, with all its frankincense, a fire–offering for the Eternal.

Leviticus 2:11–16

*A*nd if his offering be a peace–sacrifice: if he offers from the cattle, whether male or female, he is to offer it unblemished before the Eternal. He is to lay his hand on the head of his offering and slaughter it by the entrance of the tent of meeting. Aaron's sons, the priests, will sprinkle the blood around on the altar. The peace–sacrifice is to be offered as a fire–offering to the Eternal: the fat that covers the innards and all the fat which is on the innards. The two kidneys and the fat which is on them, on the flanks, and the gland over the liver, above the kidneys he is to remove. Aaron's sons will incinerate it on the altar with the ascension–offering which is on the wood, on the fire, a fire–offering, a pleasing aroma for the Eternal.

Leviticus 3:1–5

*A*nd if his offering for a peace–sacrifice for the Eternal be from the sheep, male or female, he is to offer it unblemished. And if he offers a lamb for his offering, he is to offer it before the Eternal. He is to lay his hand on the head of his offering and slaughter it by the entrance of the tent of meeting. Aaron's sons will sprinkle its blood around on the altar. From the peace–sacrifice, a fire–offering will be offered to the Eternal. He is to remove its fat, the entire rump opposite the spine, and the fat which covers the innards, all the fat which is on the innards. The two kidneys and the fat which is on them, on the flanks, and the gland over the liver above the kidneys he is to remove. The priest will incinerate it on the altar as bread of a fire–offering for the Eternal.

Leviticus 3:6–11

◇   ◇   ◇

And if his offering be a goat, he is to offer it before the Eternal. He is to lay his hand on its head and slaughter it before the tent of meeting. Aaron's sons will sprinkle its blood around on the altar. He is to offer his offering from it, a fire–offering to the Eternal: the fat which covers the innards and all the fat which is on the innards. The two kidneys and the fat which is on them, on the flanks, and the gland over the liver above the kidneys he is to remove. The priest will incinerate them on the altar as bread of a fire–offering for a pleasing aroma. All fat is for the Eternal. An everlasting decree for your generations, in all of your settlements: Do not eat any fat or any blood.

Leviticus 3:12–17

◇   ◇   ◇

Speak to the children of Israel, saying: A person who sins in ignorance of any of the Eternal's commandments concerning things which are forbidden, yet commits one of them: if the anointed priest sins, incriminating the people, he is to offer an unblemished young bull to the Eternal as a sin–offering for his sin which he has committed. He is to bring the bull to the entrance of the tent of meeting, before the Eternal. He is to lay his hand on the head of the bull and slaughter the bull before the Eternal. The anointed priest is to take from the blood of the bull and bring it to the tent of meeting. The priest is to dip his finger in the blood and splash from the blood seven times, before the Eternal, in front of the veil of the sanctuary. The priest is to put from the blood onto the horns of the altar of spicy incense, which is in the tent of meeting, before the Eternal. And he is to pour all the blood of the bull at the foundation of the ascension altar which is by the entrance of the tent of meeting. And he is to raise all the fat of the bull of the sin–offering from it: the fat that covers the innards and all the fat that is on the innards. The two kidneys and the fat which is on them, on the flanks, and the gland that is over the liver above the kidneys he is to remove—just as the peace–sacrifice was raised from the ox. The priest will incinerate them on the ascension altar. He will take the entire bull—the skin of the bull and all its meat, with its head and with its legs, its innards and its excrement—outside the camp to a pure place, to the ash dump, and burn it on wood in fire. It is to be burnt on the ash dump.

Leviticus 4:2–12

And if the entire congregation of Israel errs, and the thing is hidden from the eyes of the assembly, but they have gone against any one of the Eternal's commandments concerning a thing which has been forbidden, and are incriminated: if the sin which they have committed is known, the assembly is to offer a young bull for a sin–offering and bring it before the tent of meeting. The elders of the assembly are to lay their hands on the head of the bull, before the Eternal, and slaughter the bull before the Eternal. The anointed priest is to bring some of the blood of the bull to the tent of meeting. The priest is to dip his finger in the blood and splash it seven times, before the Eternal, in front of the veil. And he is to put some blood onto the horns of the altar which is before the Eternal, in the tent of meeting. And he is to pour all the blood at the foundation of the ascension altar which is by the entrance of the tent of meeting. And he is to raise all of its fat from it and incinerate it on the altar. He is to prepare for the bull as he prepared for the bull of the sin–offering, likewise will he prepare it. The priest will atone for them, and they will be forgiven. He will take the bull outside the camp and burn it as he burned the first bull. It is the assembly's sin–offering.

Leviticus 4:13–21

A leader who sins in ignorance and goes against any one of the commandments of the Eternal his God concerning a thing which is forbidden, and is incriminated: if his sin which he has committed is known to him, he is to bring his offering, an unblemished, male, kid goat. He is to put his hand on the head of the kid and slaughter it in the place where he would slaughter the ascension–offering, before the Eternal. It is a sin–offering. The priest is to take of the blood of the sin–offering on his finger and put it on the horns of the ascension altar. And he is to pour its blood at the foundation of the ascension altar and incinerate all its fat on the altar, just like the fat of the peace sacrifice. The priest will atone for his sin, and he will be forgiven.

Leviticus 4:22–26

◇   ◇   ◇

And if anybody among the common people sins in ignorance by going against one of the commandments concerning a thing which is forbidden, and is incriminated: if his sin which he has committed is known to him, he is to bring his offering, an unblemished, female, kid goat, for his sin which he has committed. He is to lay his hand on the head of the sin–offering and slaughter the sin–offering in the place of the ascension–offering. The priest is to take from its blood on his finger and put it on the horns of the ascension altar. And he is to pour all its blood at the foundation of the altar. And he is to remove all its fat, as the fat from the peace sacrifice was removed. The priest is to incinerate it on the altar as a pleasing aroma for the Eternal. The priest will atone for him, and he will be forgiven. And if he brings a lamb for his offering of a sin–offering, he is to bring an unblemished female. He is to lay his hand on the head of the sin–offering and slaughter it as a sin–offering, in the place where he would slaughter the ascension–offering. The priest is to take of the blood of the sin–offering on his finger and put it on the horns of the ascension altar. And he is to pour all of its blood at the foundation of the altar. And he is to remove all of its fat, as the lamb's fat would be removed from the peace sacrifice. The priest is to incinerate them on the altar, like the fire–offerings for the Eternal. The priest will atone for him, for his sin which he has sinned, and he will be forgiven.

Leviticus 4:27–35

◇   ◇   ◇

And if a person sins: if he hears the voice of an oath and is a witness, whether he saw or knew, yet he does not tell, and he bears his offense; or if a soul touches anything impure, whether the carcass of an impure animal, the carcass of an unclean beast, or the carcass of an unclean insect, and it was hidden from him, yet he is impure and is incriminated; or if he touches a man's impurity, for any of his impurities in which he may become impure, and it was hidden from him, yet it becomes known and he is incriminated; or if a soul swears, uttering with his lips for evil or for good, for anything a man may utter in an oath, and it was hidden by him, yet it becomes known, and he is incriminated for one of these: it will be when he is incriminated for one of these, that he who has sinned is to confess and bring his guilt–offering for the Eternal, for his sin which he has committed, a female from the flock, a ewe-lamb or a kid goat, as a sin–offering. The priest is to atone for him, for his sin. But if he cannot afford a lamb, he who has sinned is to bring his guilt–offering, two doves or two young pigeons for the Eternal, one for a sin–offering and one for an ascension–offering. He is to bring them to the priest and offer that which is for the sin–offering first. He is to pinch its head off its neck, but not asunder. He is to splash of the blood of the sin–offering on the wall of the altar and squeeze out the remainder of the blood at the foundation of the altar. It is a sin–offering. Then, he is to prepare the second as an ascension–offering, as customary. The priest will atone for him, for his sin which he has committed, and he will be forgiven. But if he cannot afford two doves or two pigeons, he who has sinned is to bring his offering, a tenth of a bushel of flour, as a sin–offering. He may not place oil on it and may not put frankincense on it, because it is a sin–offering. He is to bring it to the priest. The priest is to take a handful from it, a full handful, its memorial–portion, and incinerate it on the altar with the fire–offerings of the Eternal. It is a sin–offering. The priest will atone for him, for the sin which he has committed, by one of these, and he will be forgiven. It will belong to the priest as a meal–offering.

Leviticus 5:1–13

*I*f a person commits a transgression and sins in ignorance of the Eternal's sanctifications, he is to bring his guilt–offering for the Eternal, an unblemished ram from the flock, of your value of silver shekels, in holy shekels, for a guilt–offering. And he who has sinned concerning the sanctifications will pay and add its fifth in excess of it, and give it to the priest. And the priest will atone for him with the ram of the guilt–offering, and he will be forgiven. And if, when a soul sins and does any one of the Eternal's commandments which is forbidden, and he did not know it, but is incriminated and bears his offense, he is to bring an unblemished ram from the flock at your value for a guilt–offering, to the priest. The priest will atone for him, for his error which he has committed unknowingly, and he will be forgiven. It is a guilt–offering. He has been guilty—guilty to the Eternal.

Leviticus 5:15–19

If a person sins and commits a transgression against the Eternal and withholds from his companion a deposit or a loan, steals, extorts his colleague, finds what was lost and denies it, or swears falsely about any one thing that a man may sin thereby: because he has sinned and has been incriminated, he is to restore the goods which he has stolen, the extortion which he has extorted, the deposit which has been deposited with him, whatever was lost which he has found, or all upon which he has sworn falsely, and he is to pay him its principal and add an additional fifth. He is to give it to whom it belongs, on the day of his incrimination. He is to bring his guilt–offering for the Eternal, an unblemished ram from the flock, at your value of a guilt–offering, to the priest. The priest will atone for him before the Eternal, and he will be forgiven for any one thing he may have done to be incriminated.

Leviticus 5:21–26

◇ ◇ ◇

*C*ommand Aaron and his sons, saying: This is the law of the ascension–offering. It is the ascension–offering on the hearth of the altar, the fire of the altar blazing in it all night, until morning. The priest is to wear his linen shirt and wear his linen pants on his flesh. He is to raise the ash which the fire has consumed, the ascension–offering on the altar, and put it beside the altar. He is to strip his garments and don other garments. He is to take the ash outside of the camp to a pure place. Yet the fire on the altar, blazing in it, is not to be extinguished. The priest is to burn wood on it every morning. He is to arrange the ascension–offering on it and incinerate the fats of the peace–offerings on it. The perpetual fire, blazing on the altar, is not to be extinguished.

Leviticus 6:2–6

◇ ◇ ◇

*A*nd this is the law of the meal–offering. Aaron's sons are to offer it before the Eternal, in front of the altar. He (the presiding priest) is to raise, by his handful, some of the flour of the meal–offering and some of its oil, and all the frankincense which is on the meal–offering, and incinerate it on the altar as a pleasing aroma, a memorial–portion for the Eternal. And Aaron and his sons are to eat the remainder of it. Unleavened bread is to be eaten in a holy place. They are to eat it within the enclosure of the tent of meeting. Do not bake leaven. I have given them their portion from my fire–offering. It is the holiest of holies, like the sin–offering and like the guilt–offering. Every male among Aaron's children is to eat it—an everlasting decree throughout your generations, from the fire–offerings of the Eternal. All that touches them will be holy.

Leviticus 6:7–11

◇ ◇ ◇

*T*his is the offering that Aaron and his sons are to present on the day of their anointing, for the Eternal: a tenth bushel of flour, a perpetual meal–offering, half of it in the morning and half of it in the evening. It is to be prepared on a frying-pan, in oil. You are to bring it sifted. You are to offer seared crumbs, a meal–offering, a pleasing aroma for the Eternal. And the priest succeeding him (Aaron), anointed from among his sons, is to prepare it, an everlasting decree for the Eternal, completely incinerated; as every priestly meal–offering—completely. It is not to be eaten.

Leviticus 6:13–16

◇ ◇ ◇

*S*peak to Aaron and to his sons, saying: This is the law of the sin–offering. You are to slaughter the sin–offering in the place where you slaughter the ascension–offering, before the Eternal. It is the holiest of holies. The priest who makes it a sin–offering will eat it. It is to be eaten in a holy place, within the enclosure of the tent of meeting. All that touches its meat will become sanctified. And if its blood splashes on the garment, you are to wash what was splashed on, in a holy place. And a clay utensil which was cooked in is to be broken. But if it was a copper utensil for cooking, then it is to be scoured and rinsed in water. Any male priest may eat it. It is the holiest of holies. But any sin–offering, the blood of which was brought to the tent of meeting to atone in the sanctuary, is not to be eaten. It must be burnt in fire.

Leviticus 6:18–23

◇ ◇ ◇

*A*nd this is the law of the guilt–offering. It is the holiest of holies. They (the priests) are to slaughter the guilt–offering in the place where they slaughter the ascension–offering. And he (the presiding priest) is to sprinkle its blood around on the altar. And he is to offer all its fat: the rump and the fat which covers the innards. The two kidneys and the fat which is on them, on the flanks, and the gland over the liver above the kidneys he is to remove. The priest is to incinerate them on the altar, a fire–offering for the Eternal. It is a guilt–offering. Every male of the priests may eat it. It is to be eaten in a holy place. It is the holiest of holies. Like the sin–offering, like the guilt–offering, there is one law for them. It belongs to the priest who atones with it. And the priest who offers a man's ascension–offering, the skin of the ascension–offering which he offers belongs to him, to the priest. And every meal–offering which is baked in an oven and any made in the stir-pot or on a frying-pan belongs to him, to the priest who offered it. But every meal–offering mixed in oil and dried belongs to all of Aaron's sons, each one alike.

Leviticus 7:1–10

◇   ◇   ◇

And this is the law of the peace–sacrifice which a person is to offer for the Eternal. If he offers it for thanksgiving, he is to offer unleavened doughs mixed in oil in addition to the thanksgiving–sacrifice, unleavened wafers anointed in oil, and doughs of sifted flour mixed in oil. He is to present his offering with loaves of leavened bread in addition to his thanksgiving–sacrifice of peace. He is to present one of every offering as a raised–offering to the Eternal. It will belong to him—to the priest who sprinkles the blood of the peace–offering. And the meat of his thanksgiving–sacrifice of peace is to be eaten on the day of its offering. Do not leave from it until morning. And if his offering of a sacrifice is a vow–offering or a voluntary–offering, it will be eaten on the day that he offers his sacrifice. And its remainder may be eaten on the morrow as well. But on the third day, the remainder of the meat of the sacrifice is to be burnt in fire. Hence, if the meat of his peace–sacrifice is to be eaten on the third day, it will not be accepted. It will not be attributed to its offerer. It will be an abomination, and the soul who eats from it will bear his sin. Moreover, the meat which touches anything impure may not be eaten. It is to be burnt in fire. Yet, the meat—anyone pure may eat meat. But the soul who eats meat from the peace–sacrifice, which is for the Eternal, while his impurity is upon him, that soul will be cut off from its people. Also, a soul who touches on anything impure, on the impurity of man, on an impure beast or on any impure abomination, and eats from the peace–sacrifice which is for the Eternal, that soul will be cut off from its people.

Leviticus 7:11–21

*S*peak to the children of Israel, saying: Do not eat any fat of an ox, lamb, or goat. Fat of a carcass or torn fat may be prepared for any work, but you must not eat it. Because anyone eating fat from a beast, from which a fire–offering to the Eternal is to be offered, for eating it, that soul will be cut off from its people. Also, do not eat any blood of a bird or of a beast in any of your settlements. Any soul who eats any blood, that soul will be cut off from its people.

Leviticus 7:23–27

◇   ◇   ◇

*S*peak to the children of Israel, saying: The offerer of his peace–sacrifice to the Eternal is to bring his offering to the Eternal from his peace–sacrifice. His hands are to bring it, the Eternal's fire–offerings. He is to bring the fat with the breast, to wave its breast as a wave–offering before the Eternal. The priest is to incinerate the fat on the altar. The breast will belong to Aaron and to his sons. And you are to give the right shank, a raised–offering from your peace–sacrifices, to the priest. The offerer, from among Aaron's sons, of the blood of the peace–offering and the fat—the right shank belongs to him as his portion. For I have taken the breast of the wave–offering and the shank of the raised–offering from the children of Israel, from their peace–sacrifices, and I have given them to Aaron the priest and to his sons as an everlasting decree from the children of Israel. This is the anointing of Aaron and the anointing of his sons from the fire–offerings of the Eternal on the day he let them approach to be priests for the Eternal, which the Eternal commanded to give them from the children of Israel on the day of his anointing them, an everlasting decree for their generations. This is the law for the ascension–offering, for the meal–offering, for the sin–offering, for the guilt–offering, for the consecration–offering, and for the peace–sacrifice, which the Eternal commanded Moses on Mount Sinai, on the day he commanded the children of Israel to offer their offerings to the Eternal, in the Sinai Desert.

Leviticus 7:29–38

◇   ◇   ◇

*T*ake Aaron and his sons with him, and the garments, the anointing oil, the bull of the sin–offering, the two rams, and the basket of unleavened bread, and assemble the entire congregation by the entrance of the tent of meeting.

Leviticus 8:2–3

*D*o not drink wine or intoxicants, you and your sons with you, when you come to the tent of meeting, so that you not die, an everlasting decree for your generations—and to separate between the holy and the profane, between the impure and the pure, and to teach the children of Israel all the decrees which the Eternal has spoken to them through the hand of Moses.

Leviticus 10:9–11

◇   ◇   ◇

*S*peak to the children of Israel, saying: These are the animals which you may eat from among all the beasts which are on the earth. Any of the beasts with split-hoof and cleft-footed hoof, chewing cud, you may eat. But this you may not eat from among the cud-chewing and from among the split-hoofed: the camel, because it chews cud, but its hoof is not split. It is impure to you. And the rabbit, because it chews cud but is not split-hoofed. It is impure to you. And the hare, because it chews cud but is not split-hoofed. It is impure to you. And the pig, because it is split-hoofed and cleft-foot hoofed, but it does not chew cud. It is impure to you. Do not eat any of their meat. And do not touch their carcass. They are impure to you. This you may eat from among all that is in the water. All that have fin and scales in the water, in the seas, and in the streams, you may eat. But all that do not have fin and scales in the seas and in the streams, of any infestation of the water and of any living being which is in the water, are detestable to you. And they will be detestable to you. You may not eat from their meat. And you will detest their carcass. All which do not have fin and scales in the water are detestable to you. And you will detest these from the fowl. They may not be eaten. They are detestable: the eagle, the vulture, the osprey, the falcon, the buzzard of its kind, any raven of its kind, the ostrich, the kite, the sea gull, the hawk of its kinds, the owlet, the cormorant, the owl, the barn-owl, the pelican, the crane, the stork, the heron of its kind, the hoopoe, and the bat. Any winged insect which walks on four is detestable to you. But this you may eat from any winged insect which walks on four, which has legs above its feet to jump with on the ground. You may eat of these: the locust of its kind, the cicada of its kind, the cricket of its kind, and the grasshopper of its kind. But every winged insect which has four feet is detestable to you.

Leviticus 11:2–23

And for these you will be rendered impure. All who touch their carcass will be impure until the evening. And all who carry from their carcass will wash their garments and be impure until the evening. Any beast whose hoof is split but whose foot is not cleft, and does not chew cud, is impure to you. All who touch them will be rendered impure. And any that walk on their paws, of any of the animals which walk on four, are impure to you. All who touch their carcass will be rendered impure until the evening. Therefore, the bearer of their carcass is to wash his garments and be considered impure until the evening. They are impure to you. And this is the impure to you of the creature which creeps on the ground: the rat, the mouse, the turtle of its kind, the ferret, the chameleon, the lizard, the reptile, and the mole. These are the impure to you of all which creep. All who touch them, when they are dead, will be rendered impure until the evening. Also, everything on which they fall while they are dead will be rendered impure. Every wooden vessel, cloth, hide, or sack, any utensil in which work is done, is to be brought into water and considered impure until the evening, and then be purified. And any clay vessel into which they fall, all that is in it will become impure, and you are to destroy it. All the food which may be eaten, on which water comes, will become impure. And all drink which is drunk in any vessel will become impure. Also, all on which their carcass falls will be rendered impure. An oven and a stove will be demolished. They are impure, and they will be considered impure by you. But a spring and a cistern collecting water will still be pure. Yet, what touches their carcass will be impure. Also, if their carcass has fallen on any sowing seed which may be sown, it is pure. But if a seed has been watered and their carcass falls on it, it is impure to you.

Leviticus 11:24–38

And if any of the beasts which are for you to eat, dies, the handler of its carcass will be rendered impure until the evening. And the eater from its carcass is to wash his garments and be considered impure until evening. And the lifter of its carcass is to wash his garments and be considered impure until the evening. Also, every creature which creeps on the ground is detestable. It may not be eaten. All going on their belly and all walking on four, including all the multiple-legged of every creature which creeps on the ground may not be eaten, because they are detestable. Do not make your souls detestable by any creature which creeps. And do not become impure by them and unclean by them, for I am the Eternal your God. Sanctify yourselves and be holy, for I am holy. Therefore, do not make your souls impure with any infestation which creeps over the ground, for I am the Eternal who brings you up from the land of Egypt to be God to you. You are to be holy, because I am holy. This is the law of the beast, the fowl, every living being which infests the waters, and every being which creeps on the ground, to separate between the impure and the pure, and between the animal which is to be eaten and the animal which is not to be eaten.

Leviticus 11:39–47

◇   ◇   ◇

*S*peak to the children of Israel, saying: If a woman conceives and bears a male, she will be considered impure for seven days. As on the days of her period of menstruation, she will be impure. And on the eighth day, the flesh of his foreskin will be circumcised. And she is to remain in the blood of her purification for thirty days and three days. She may not touch anything sanctified and is not to come to the sanctuary until the days of her purification are culminated. And if she bears a female, she will be considered impure for two weeks, as it is for her period. And she is to remain with the blood of her purification for sixty-six days. And when the days of her purification are culminated, for a son or for a daughter, she is to bring a year-old lamb for an ascension–offering and a young pigeon or dove for a sin–offering to the entrance of the tent of meeting, to the priest. He is to offer it before the Eternal, to atone for her. She will be purified from the source of her blood. This is the law of the bearer of a male or of a female. But if she cannot afford a lamb, she is to take two doves or two young pigeons, one for an ascension–offering and one for a sin–offering. The priest will atone for her, and she will be purified.

Leviticus 12:2–8

*I*f a man has a swelling, a rash, or a blister on his skin, and it is in the skin of his flesh like the infection of leprosy, he is to come to Aaron the priest or to one of his sons, the priests. The priest will see the infection in the skin of his flesh. If the hair in the infection has turned white, and the infection appears deeper than the skin of his flesh, it is an infection of leprosy. The priest will see him and declare him impure. And if it is a white blister in the skin of his flesh but does not appear deeper than the skin, and its hair has not turned white, the priest is to quarantine the infected one for seven days. On the seventh day, the priest is to see him. If here, the infection ceases in his sight, and the infection has not spread in the skin, the priest is to quarantine him again for seven days. The priest is to see him on the seventh day again. If here, the infection is fading, and the infection has not spread in the skin, the priest will declare him pure. It is a rash. He is to wash his garments and be purified. But if the rash spreads and spreads in the skin after the priest sees him to declare him pure, he is to be seen by the priest again. As the priest sees that here the rash has spread in the skin, the priest will declare him impure. It is leprosy.

Leviticus 13:1–8

When the infection of leprosy is in a man, he is to come to the priest. The priest will see that here is a white swelling in the skin, and it has turned the hair white, and raw flesh lives in the swelling. It is chronic leprosy in the skin of his flesh. The priest is to declare him impure. He is not to quarantine him, because he is impure. But if the leprosy bursts and bursts in the skin, so the leprosy covers all of the infected skin, from his head until his feet, in all appearance to the eyes of the priest, and the priest sees that here the leprosy covers all of his flesh, he will declare the infection pure. All of it having turned white, it is pure. But on the day when living flesh appears in it, it will be considered impure. The priest will see the living flesh and declare it impure. The living flesh is impure. It is leprosy. Or if the living flesh returns but turns white, and he comes to the priest, and the priest sees him, that here the infection has turned white, the priest will declare the infection pure. It is pure.

Leviticus 13:9–17

And if a boil is in the flesh of his skin and heals, and in place of the boil is a white swelling or a reddish-white blister, and it is shown to the priest, and the priest sees, here, that it appears deeper than the skin, and its hair has turned white, the priest is to declare him impure. It is an infection of leprosy bursting in a boil. But if the priest sees it, and here, white hair is not in it, and it is not deeper than the skin, and it is fading, the priest is to quarantine him for seven days. Then, if it spreads and spreads in the skin, the priest will declare him impure. He is infected. But if the blister ceases in its place, not spreading, it is the scar of a boil. The priest is to declare him pure. Or if a fire-burns is in the flesh of his skin, and the tissue of the burn has a blister, reddish-white or white, and the priest sees it, and here, hair has turned white in the blister, and it appears deeper than the skin: it is leprosy bursting in a burn. The priest is to declare him impure. It is an infection of leprosy. But if the priest sees it, and here, white hair is not in the blister, and it is not deeper than the skin, and it is fading, the priest is to quarantine him for seven days. The priest is to see him on the seventh day. If it has spread and spread in the skin, the priest is to declare him impure. It is an infection of leprosy. But if the blister ceases in its place, not spreading in the skin, and it is fading: it is a swelling of the burn. The priest is to declare him pure, because it is a scar of the burn.

Leviticus 13:18–28

And a man or a woman who has an infection on him, on the head or on the beard, and the priest sees the infection, and here it appears deeper than the skin, and thin yellow hair is in it, the priest is to declare him impure. It is psoriasis. It is leprosy of the head or the beard. But if the priest sees the infection of psoriasis, and here, it does not appear deeper than the skin, and there is no black hair in it, the priest is to quarantine the psoriasis-infected one for seven days. The priest will see the infected one on the seventh day, and here, the psoriasis has not spread and does not have yellow hair in it, and the psoriasis does not appear deeper than the skin. Therefore, he will shave, but he may not shave the psoriasis. The priest is to quarantine the psoriasis again for seven days. The priest is to see the psoriasis on the seventh day, and here, the psoriasis has not spread in the skin and does not appear deeper than the skin. Therefore, the priest will declare him pure. He is to wash his clothes and be pure. But if the psoriasis spreads and spreads in the skin after he is declared pure, and the priest sees him, and here the psoriasis has spread in the skin, the priest is not to inspect for the yellow hair. He is impure. But if the psoriasis ceases in his eyes, and black hair grows in it, the psoriasis is healed. He is pure. The priest is to declare him pure.

Leviticus 13:29–37

And if a man or a woman has pocks, white pocks in the skin of his flesh, and the priest sees that here are faint pocks in the skin of his flesh: it is albinism bursting in the skin. He is pure. And a man whose head is plucked, he is bald. He is pure. And if his head is plucked from the corner of his face, he is bald foreheaded. He is pure. But if a bald head or a bald forehead has a reddish-white infection, it is leprosy bursting in his bald head or in his bald forehead. The priest is to see him, and if here, the swelling of the infection is reddish-white in his bald head or in his bald forehead, like the appearance of leprosy of the skin of the flesh, he is a leprous man. He is impure. The priest must declare him impure. His infection is on his head. And the leper who has the infection, his clothes are to be stripped, and his head is to be dishevelled and wrapped until his mustache, and he is to call out: Impure! Impure! He will be declared impure all the days that the infection is on him. He is impure. He is to sit alone. His habitation is outside the camp.

Leviticus 13:38–46

◇   ◇   ◇

And the garment which has the infection of leprosy in it, in a woolen garment or in a linen garment, whether in the warp or in the woof of linen or of wool, or in leather, or in any leather-work, and the infection is greenish or reddish in the garment, or in the leather, whether in the warp or in the woof or in any leather utensil, it is an infection of leprosy and should be seen by the priest. The priest is to see the infection and quarantine the infection for seven days. The priest will see the infection on the seventh day. If the infection has spread in the garment, whether in the warp or in the woof or in leather, for any work of leather that may be made, the infection is a malignant leprosy. It is impure. The garment, whether warp or woof of wool or linen or any leather utensil which the infection is in, is to be burnt, because it is a malignant leprosy. It is to be burnt in fire. But if the priest sees that here, the infection has not spread in the garment, whether in the warp or in the woof or in any leather utensil, the priest is to command that they wash what the infection is in. He is to quarantine it again for seven days. The priest will see the infection after it has been washed: if here the infection has not changed its appearance, even though the infection has not spread, it is impure. Burn it in fire. It is sunken in its worn-patches and in its bald-patches. But if the priest sees that here the infection has faded after washing it, he is to tear it from the garment or from the leather, whether from the warp or from the woof. Then, if it is still seen in the garment, whether in the warp or in the woof or in any leather utensil, it is spreading. Burn what the infection is in with fire. But the garment, whether the warp or the woof or any leather utensil you may wash, from which the infection has been removed, wash it again and declare it pure. This is the law of the infection of leprosy of the woolen or linen garment, of the warp or of the woof or of any leather utensil, for its purity or for its impurity.

Leviticus 13:47–59

*T*his will be the law of the leper on the day of his being purified and brought to the priest. The priest is to go outside the camp. The priest is to see whether the infection of leprosy in the leper has healed. The priest will command, and he is to take two pure, live birds, cedar wood, scarlet-crimson, and hyssop for the purification. The priest will command, and he is to slaughter the first bird in a clay vessel over running water. He is to take the live bird, the cedar wood, the scarlet-crimson, and the hyssop, and dip them and the live bird in the blood of the slaughtered bird, over running water. He is to splash seven times on him who is purified from the leprosy and declare him pure. He is to send the live bird out over the field. The purified one is to wash his clothes, shave all of his hair, bathe in water, and be purified. And afterwards, he will come to the camp and sit outside his tent for seven days. On the seventh day, he is to shave all the hair of his head, his beard, and his eyebrows. Hence, he will shave all his hair, wash his clothes, bathe his flesh in water, and be considered pure. And on the eighth day, he is to take two unblemished lambs, one unblemished year-old ewe, three tenths of flour mixed in oil as a meal–offering, and one liter of oil. The priest who is purifying is to stand them and the man to be purified before the Eternal, by the entrance of the tent of meeting. The priest is to take the first lamb and offer it as a guilt–offering, and the liter of oil. He is to wave them as a wave–offering before the Eternal. He is to slaughter the lamb in a place where he would slaughter the sin–offering and the ascension–offering, in a sanctified place, because the guilt–offering is like the sin–offering for the priest. It is the holiest of holies. The priest is to take from the blood of the guilt–offering, and the priest is to put it on the right ear lobe of the purified one, on the thumb of his right hand, and on the thumb of his right foot. The priest is to take from the liter of oil and pour on the priest's left palm. The priest is to dip his right finger into the oil which is on his left palm and splash some of the oil, with his finger, seven times before the Eternal. And the priest is to put some of the remaining oil, which is on his palm, on the right ear lobe of the purified one, on the thumb of his right hand, and on the thumb of his right foot, over the blood of the guilt–offering. And the priest is to put the remainder of the oil, which is on his palm, on the head of the purified one. The priest will atone for him before the Eternal. The priest is to prepare the sin–offering, atone for the purified one from his impurity, and afterwards, slaughter the ascension–offering. The priest is to raise the ascension–offering and the meal–offering on the altar. The priest will atone for him, and he will be rendered pure. But if he is needy and his hand cannot afford, he is to take one lamb, a guilt–offering for waving, as atonement for him, one tenth of flour mixed in oil as a meal–offering, a liter of oil, and two doves or two young pigeons—what he can afford. One will be a sin–offering and one an ascension–offering. He is to bring them, on the eighth day of his purification, to the priest, by the entrance of the tent of meeting, before the Eternal. The priest is to take the lamb of the guilt–offering and the liter of oil, and the priest is to wave them as a wave–offering before the Eternal. He is to slaughter the lamb of the guilt–offering. The priest is to take some of the blood of the guilt–offering and put it on the right ear lobe of the purified one, on the thumb of his right hand, and on the thumb of his right foot. The priest is to pour some of the oil onto the priest's left palm. The priest is to splash, with his right finger, the oil which is on his left palm, seven times, before the Eternal. The priest is to put some of the oil, which is on his palm, on the right ear lobe of the purified one, on the thumb of his right hand, and on the thumb of his right foot, over the place of the blood of the guilt–offering. And he is to put the remainder of the oil, which is on the priest's palm, on the head of the purified one, to atone for him before the Eternal. He is to prepare one from the doves or from the young pigeons, according to what he can afford; according to what he can afford—the one for a sin–offering and the one for an ascension–offering, with the meal–offering. The priest will atone for the purified one before the Eternal. This is the law for whoever has the infection of leprosy, who cannot afford his purification.

Leviticus 14:2–32

◇   ◇   ◇

When you come to the land of Canaan, which I give you for possession, and I put the infection of leprosy in a house in the land of your possession, and he whose house it is comes to tell the priest, saying: "It looks to me as though an infection is in the house," the priest is to command that they empty the house before the priest comes to see the infection, so that all in the house not be declared impure. And afterwards, the priest is to come to see the house and to see the infection. And, if here, the infection is in the walls of the house, greenish or reddish depressions, and their appearance is deeper than the wall, the priest is to go out of the house, to the entrance of the house, and quarantine the house for seven days. The priest is to return on the seventh day and see if here the infection has spread in the walls. The priest is then to command that they remove the infected stones and throw them outside the city to an impure place. And he is to scrape around inside the house, and they are to pour the dust, which they scraped, outside the city at an impure place. They are to take other stones and bring them instead of the stones, and he is to take other dust and plaster the house. Then, if the infection returns and erupts in the house after the stones were removed, after scraping the house, and after plastering, the priest is to come and see, and if here, the infection has spread in the house, it is malignant leprosy in the house. It is impure. He is to demolish the house: its stones, its wood, and any dust of the house, and take it outside the city to an impure place. And whoever enters the house on any of the days of its quarantine will be rendered impure until the evening. And whoever lies in the house is to wash his clothes. Also, whoever eats in the house is to wash his clothes. But if the priest comes and sees that here the infection has not spread in the house after plastering the house, the priest is to declare the house pure, because the infection has healed. He is to take two birds, cedar wood, scarlet-crimson, and hyssop to purify the house. He is to slaughter the first bird in a clay vessel, over running water. He is to take the cedar wood, the hyssop, the scarlet-crimson, and the live bird, and dip them in the blood of the slaughtered bird and in the running water, and splash the house seven times. He will atone for the house with the blood of the bird, with the running water, with the live bird, with the cedar wood, with the hyssop and with the scarlet-crimson. He is to send the live bird outside the city, over the field. He will atone for the house, and it will be pure. This is the law for any infection and psoriasis, for leprosy of a garment or of a house, for a swelling, for a rash, and for a blister, to teach of the day of impurity and of the day of purity. This is the law of leprosy.

Leviticus 14:34–57

◇　◇　◇

Speak to the children of Israel and say to them: Each man who has a discharge from his flesh, his discharge is impure. And this will be his impurity from his discharge, his flesh oozing his discharge or his flesh congested by his discharge. It is his impurity. Anything for lying, upon which the discharger lies, will be rendered impure. And any article on which he sits will be rendered impure. And a man who touches his bed is to wash his clothes, bathe in water, and be rendered impure until the evening. Also, he who sits on the article upon which the discharger has sat is to wash his clothes, bathe in water, and be rendered impure until the evening. Also, he who touches of the discharger's flesh is to wash his clothes, bathe in water, and be rendered unclean until the evening. And if the discharger spits on the pure, he is to wash his clothes, bathe in water, and be rendered impure until the evening. And anything for riding, on which the discharger rides, will be rendered impure. And all who touch anything which was beneath him will be rendered impure until the evening. Also, the bearer of them is to wash his clothes, bathe in water, and be rendered impure until the evening. And whoever the discharger touches while his hands were not yet rinsed in water is to wash his clothes, bathe in water, and be rendered impure until the evening. And a clay vessel which the discharger touches is to be broken, but any wooden vessel may be rinsed in water. And when the discharger is purified from his discharge and has counted seven days for himself, for his purification, and has washed his clothes, bathed his flesh in running water, and is rendered pure, then, on the eighth day, he is to get himself two doves or two young pigeons and come before the Eternal, by the entrance of the tent of meeting. He is to give them to the priest. The priest will prepare them: one as a sin–offering and one as an ascension–offering. The priest will atone for him, before the Eternal, for his discharge.

Leviticus 15:2–15

◇   ◇   ◇

And when semen is emitted from a man, he is to bathe all of his flesh in water and be impure until the evening. And any garment or any leather which has semen on it is to be washed in water and be impure until the evening. And a woman with whom a man lies and has a seminal emission, they too are to bathe in water and be impure until the evening. And a woman who has a discharge, her discharge from her flesh being of blood, is to be in her period for seven days. And anything which touches her will be impure until evening. And anything upon which she lies during her period is to be considered impure. And anything upon which she sits is to be considered impure. And anyone who touches her bed is to wash his clothes, bathe in water, and be impure until the evening. And anyone who touches any article on which she has sat is to wash his clothes, bathe in water, and be impure until the evening. And, if he is on the bed or on the article upon which she has sat, and he touches it, he will be impure until the evening. And, if a man lies with her, so that her period is on him, he is to be considered impure for seven days. And anything for lying, upon which he lies, is to be considered impure. And if a woman discharges a discharge of blood for many days, not in the time of her period, or if she discharges past her period, all the days of her discharge of impurity are to be like the days of her period. She is impure. Any bed upon which she lies any day of her discharge is to be to her like the bed of her period. And any article upon which she sits will be considered impure, as the impurity of her period. And anyone who touches them will be impure, wash his clothes, bathe in water, and be impure until the evening. And when she is purified of her discharge, she is to count, for herself, seven days, and afterwards she will be purified. And on the eighth day, she is to get herself two doves or two young pigeons and bring them to the priest, to the entrance of the tent of meeting. The priest is to prepare one as the sin–offering and one as the ascension–offering. The priest is to atone for her before the Eternal, for the discharge of her impurity. The children of Israel are to abstain in their impurity and not die in their impurity by making my tabernacle, which is in their midst, impure. This is the law of the discharger and of him who emits semen, being impure by it, and of the menstruant in her period, and of the discharger of his discharge, for male and for female, and for the man who lies with impurity.

Leviticus 15:16–33

◊   ◊   ◊

Speak to Aaron, your brother, that he not come at any time into the sanctuary inside the veil, in front of the covering which is over the ark, so as not to die. Because, I will be seen in a cloud over the covering. Aaron is to come to the sanctuary with this: a young bull for a sin–offering and a ram for an ascension–offering. He is to wear a sanctified linen shirt and breechcloths on his flesh, and he is to be girded with a linen belt and wrapped with a linen turban. They are the sanctified garments. He is to bathe his flesh in water and wear them. Then, he is to take two kid goats from the congregation of the children of Israel for a sin–offering and one ram for an ascension–offering. Aaron will offer a bull which is his for the sin–offering and atone for himself and for the sake of his house. He is to take the two kids and stand them up before the Eternal, by the entrance of the tent of meeting. Aaron is to put lots on the two kids: one lot for the Eternal and one lot for Azazel. Aaron will offer the kid on which arose the lot for the Eternal and prepare it as a sin–offering. But the kid on which the lot for Azazel arose is to stand alive before the Eternal, for atonement, to be cast to Azazel, to the desert. Aaron is to offer the bull of the sin–offering, which is his, and atone for himself and for the sake of his house. He is to slaughter the bull, which is his. He is to take a censer full of flaming coals from the altar, from before the Eternal, and full handfuls of fine, spicy incense, and bring it behind the veil. He is to put the incense on the fire, before the Eternal. The cloud of incense will obscure the covering which is over the testimony, so he will not die. He is to take blood of the bull and splash the covering with his finger, eastwards. He is to splash the blood with his finger seven times before the covering. He is to slaughter the kid of the sin—offering which is for the people, bring its blood inside the veil, and do with its blood just as he did with the blood of the bull. He is to splash it on the covering and in front of the covering. He will atone for the sanctuary, for the impurity of the children of Israel, for their crimes, and for all their sins. And so will he do for the tent of meeting which dwells with them, amidst their impurity. No man is to be in the tent of meeting when he comes to atone for the sanctuary, until he goes out and atones for himself, for the sake of his house and for the sake of all of the assembly of Israel. He is to go out to the altar which is before the Eternal and atone for it. He is to take the blood of the bull and the blood of the kid and put it around on the horns of the altar. He is to splash it seven times with the blood, with his finger, purify it, and sanctify it from the impurities of the children of Israel. He will finish atoning for the sanctuary, for the tent of meeting, and for the altar, and will offer the live kid. Aaron is to lay his two hands on the head of the live kid and confess over it all of the iniquities of the children of Israel and all of their crimes in all of their sins. He will put them on the head of the kid and send it, by the hand of a ready man, to the desert. The kid is to bear all of their iniquities to a desolate land. He is to send the kid into the desert. Aaron is to come to the tent of meeting and remove the linen garments which he wore when he came to the sanctuary and lay them there. He is to bathe his flesh in water in a sanctified place, don his garments, go out, and prepare his ascension—offering and the peoples' ascension—offering. He will atone for himself and for the sake of the people. And he is to incinerate the fat of the sin—offering on the altar. Then, he who casts the kid to Azazel is to wash his garments, bathe his flesh in water, and, afterwards, he may reenter the camp. He is to take the bull of the sin—offering and the kid of the sin—offering, the blood of which was brought to atone for the sanctuary, outside the camp. They are to burn its skins, its flesh, and its excrement in fire. And he who burns them is to wash his garments, bathe his flesh in water, and afterwards, he may come into the camp. It is to be an everlasting decree for you. In the seventh month, on the tenth of the month, you are to humble your souls and do no work, the native and the foreigner who lives among you, for on this day, he will atone for you to purify you. You will be purified from all of your sins before the Eternal. It is a Sabbath of rest for you. You are to humble your souls—an everlasting decree. The priest who was anointed and whose hand was consecrated to be a priest succeeding his father is to atone and wear the linen garments, the sanctified garments. He is to atone for the holy sanctuary. And he is to atone for the tent of meeting and for the altar. And he is to atone for the priests and for all the people of the assembly. This is to be an everlasting decree for you: to atone for the children of Israel for all of their sins, once a year.

Leviticus 16:2–34

Speak to Aaron, to his sons, and to all the children of Israel, and say to them: This is the thing that the Eternal has commanded, saying: Any man from the house of Israel who slaughters an ox, a lamb, or a goat within the camp, or who slaughters outside the camp but does not bring it to the entrance of the tent of meeting to present an offering for the Eternal, before the tabernacle of the Eternal, blood will be accounted to that man. He has spilled blood. That man will be cut off from among his people: in order that the children of Israel bring their sacrifices which they sacrifice in the field, and bring them for the Eternal, to the entrance of the tent of meeting, to the priest, and sacrifice them as peace–sacrifices for the Eternal. The priest is to sprinkle the blood on the altar of the Eternal, by the entrance of the tent of meeting. He is to incinerate the fat as a pleasing aroma for the Eternal. Henceforth, they may no longer sacrifice their sacrifices to the demons whom they solicit. This is to be an everlasting decree for them, throughout their generations.

Leviticus 17:2–7

And you are to say to them: Any man from the house of Israel or foreigner who lives among you who raises an ascension–offering or a sacrifice but does not bring it to the entrance of the tent of meeting to prepare it for the Eternal, that man will be cut off from his people. And any man from the house of Israel or foreigner who lives among you who eats any blood, I will set my face against the soul who eats blood and cut it off from among its people. For the soul of the flesh is in the blood. Therefore, I have given it to you on the altar to atone for your souls, because the blood atones for the soul. Therefore, I have said to the children of Israel: Any soul among you may not eat blood. And the foreigner who lives among you may not eat blood. Also, any man from the house of Israel or foreigner who lives among you who hunts game—animal or fowl which may be eaten—is to pour out its blood and cover it with dust. For the soul of all flesh is its blood; it is with its soul. Therefore, I have said to the children of Israel: Do not eat the blood of any flesh, because the soul of all flesh is its blood. All who eat it will be cut off. Also, any soul, whether a native or a foreigner, who eats a carcass or mutilation, he is to wash his clothes and bathe in water. He will be impure until the evening and then be pure. But if he does not wash and does not bathe his flesh, he will bear his guilt.

Leviticus 17:8–16

Speak to the children of Israel and say to them: I am the Eternal, your God. Do not do as the deeds of the land of Egypt in which you were settled. And do not do as the deeds of the land of Canaan, when I bring you there. And do not go by their rules. You are to do my judgments and safeguard my decrees, to go by them. I am the Eternal your God. You are to safeguard my decrees and my judgments, those which a man may do, and live by them. I am the Eternal. No man may approach any kin of his flesh to uncover nakedness. I am the Eternal. Do not uncover the nakedness of your father or of your mother. She is your mother. Do not uncover her nakedness. Do not uncover the nakedness of your father's wife. It is your father's nakedness. The nakedness of your sister, your father's daughter or your mother's daughter, born at home or born away—do not uncover their nakedness. The nakedness of your son's daughter or your daughter's daughter—do not uncover their nakedness, because they are your nakedness. The nakedness of your father's wife's daughter, born to your father, she is your sister. Do not uncover her nakedness. Do not uncover the nakedness of your father's sister. She is your father's kin. Do not uncover the nakedness of your mother's sister, because she is your mother's kin. Do not uncover the nakedness of your father's brother. Do not approach his wife. She is your aunt. Do not uncover the nakedness of your daughter-in-law. She is your son's wife. Do not uncover her nakedness. Do not uncover the nakedness of your brother's wife. It is your brother's nakedness. Do not uncover the nakedness of a woman and her daughter. Do not take her son's daughter or her daughter's daughter to uncover her nakedness. They are kin. It is incest. And do not take a wife with her sister, for rivalry, to uncover her nakedness and hers during her life. And do not approach to uncover the nakedness of a woman during the period of her impurity. And do not give your bed and seed to your fellow-man's wife, to become impure with her. And do not give your children to be passed to Moloch. Thereby, you will not profane the name of your God. I am the Eternal.

Leviticus 18:2–21

And do not lie, as a woman lies, with a male. It is an abomination. And do not bed with any beast, to become impure with it. And a woman may not stand before a beast to copulate. It is a perversion. Do not become impure with any of these; because the nations, which I cast out before you, are impure with all these. Hence, the land is impure. Therefore, I will punish its iniquity on it, and the land will vomit its inhabitants. You are to safeguard them, my decrees and my judgments, and not do any of these abominations, the native or the foreigner who lives among you, because the men of the land which is before you have done all of these abominations and have made the land impure. Then, the land will not vomit you for making it impure, as it vomited the nations which were before you. Because all who do any of these abominations, the souls that do it will be cut off from among their people. You are to safeguard my observances in order not to do the abominable acts which were done before you. And you are not to become impure by them. I am the Eternal your God.

Leviticus 18:22–30

Speak to the entire congregation of the children of Israel and say to them: You will be holy, because I, the Eternal your God, am holy. A man is to fear his mother and father. And you are to safeguard my Sabbaths. I am the Eternal your God. Do not turn to idols. And do not make molten gods for yourselves. I am the Eternal your God. And when you sacrifice a peace–sacrifice for the Eternal, sacrifice it for your acceptance. It is to be eaten on the day of your sacrifice and on the morrow; and the remainder up to the third day is to be burnt in fire. But indeed, if it is to be eaten on the third day, it is an abomination. It will not be accepted. And he who eats it will bear his sin, because he has profaned the holiness of the Eternal. That soul will be cut off from its people. And when you harvest the harvest of your land, do not finish harvesting the corner of your field. And do not glean the gleaning of your harvest. Also, do not despoil your vineyard or glean the spoils of your vineyard. Abandon them for the poor and for the stranger. I am the Eternal your God. A man is not to steal, not to deceive, and not to lie to his fellow-man. And do not swear by my name falsely, profaning the name of your God. I am the Eternal. Do not extort your acquaintance. And do not steal. Do not retain the wages of a laborer with you until the morning. Do not curse the deaf or put an obstacle before the blind, but fear your God. I am the Eternal. Do not cause an injustice in judgment. Do not favor the needy. And do not glorify the great. You are to judge your fellow-man with righteousness. Do not go slandering among your people. Do not stand over the blood of your acquaintance. I am the Eternal. Do not hate your brother in your heart. You must admonish your fellow-man and not bear his sin. Do not avenge. And do not begrudge the children of your people. You are to love your neighbor as yourself. I am the Eternal.

Leviticus 19:2–18

*Y*ou are to safeguard my decrees. Do not crossbreed your cattle. Do not cross-seed your field. And do not put a cross-woven woolen-linen garment on yourself. And if a man lies with a woman, emitting semen, while she is a servant betrothed to a man, and she has not been redeemed for redemption, or freedom has not been given to her, there is to be an inquiry. They are not to die, for she was not free. He is to bring his guilt–offering for the Eternal, to the entrance of the tent of meeting, a ram for a guilt–offering. The priest will atone for him with the ram of the guilt–offering, before the Eternal, for his sin which he has sinned. He will be forgiven from his sin which he has sinned. And when you come to the land and plant any edible tree, let them be unpruned. Let their fruit be unpruned. Let it be unprunable to you for three years. It is not to be eaten. Then, in the fourth year, all of its fruit will be sanctified, praiseworthy for the Eternal. And in the fifth year, you may eat its fruit—to increase its yield for you. I am the Eternal your God. Do not eat with blood. Do not divine. Do not soothsay. Do not round the corners of your head. And do not shave the corners of your beard. Do not put an incision in your flesh for the dead. And do not put tattoo writing on yourselves. I am the Eternal. Do not defile your daughter, to let her solicit; hence, the land will not solicit and the land become filled with incest. You are to safeguard my Sabbaths and fear my sanctuary. I am the Eternal. Do not turn to the sorcerers. And do not seek for the necromancers, to become impure with them. I am the Eternal your God. You are to rise before the aged, glorify the old, and be afraid of your God. I am the Eternal. And if a foreigner lives with you in your land, do not torment him. The foreigner who lives with you is to be to you as the native among you. You are to love him as yourself, because you were foreigners in the land of Egypt. I am the Eternal your God. Do not do injustice in judgment—in measure, in weight, or in quantity. Have correct scales, correct stones, a correct bushel, and a correct gallon. I am the Eternal your God who brought you out from the land of Egypt. Safeguard all of my decrees and all of my judgments, and do them. I am the Eternal.

Leviticus 19:19–37

*T*herefore, say to the children of Israel: Any man among the children of Israel or among the foreigners who live in Israel, who gives his children to Moloch must die. The people of the land are to cast stones at him. And I will oppose that man and cut him off from among his people, because he has given his children to Moloch, causing my sanctuary to become impure and profaning my holy name. But if the people of the land disregard that man when he gives his children to Moloch so as not to kill him, I will oppose that man and his family and cut him off and all who solicit after him, to solicit after Moloch, from among their people. Also, the soul who turns to the sorcerers or to the necromancers, to solicit after them, I will oppose that man and cut him off from among his people. Sanctify yourselves and be holy, for I am the Eternal your God. Safeguard my decrees and do them. I am the Eternal your sanctifier.

Leviticus 20:2–8

◇   ◇   ◇

*A*ny man who curses his father or his mother must die. He has cursed his father or his mother. His blood is on him. And a man who commits adultery with the wife of a man, who commits adultery with the wife of his acquaintance, the adulterer and the adulteress must die. And a man who lies with the wife of his father has uncovered his father's nakedness. The two of them must die. Their blood is on them. And a man who lies with his daughter-in-law, the two of them must die. The have done a perversion. Their blood is on them. And a man who lies as a woman lies, with a male, the two of them have done an abomination. They must die. Their blood is on them. And a man who takes a wife and her mother, it is incest. He and they are to be burnt in fire. Then incest will not be among you. And a man who makes his bed with a beast must die. And you are to kill the beast. And a woman who approaches any beast to copulate with it, you are to kill the woman and the beast. They must die. Their blood is on them. And a man who takes his sister, his father's daughter or his mother's daughter, and sees her nakedness, and she sees his nakedness, it is a disgrace. They will be cut off before the eyes of the children of their people. He has uncovered the nakedness of his sister. He will bear his sin. And a man who lies with a menstruating woman and uncovers her nakedness, exposing her source, and she uncovers the source of her blood, the two of them will be cut off from among their people. And do not uncover the nakedness of your mother's sister or your father's sister, because his kin is exposed. They will bear their guilt. And a man who lies with his aunt, he has uncovered his uncle's nakedness. They will bear their sin. They will die childless. And a man who takes his brother's wife, who is forbidden, he has uncovered his brother's nakedness. They will be childless. Safeguard all my decrees and all my judgments and do them, so the land, there where I am bringing you in to settle, will not vomit you. Therefore, do not go by the rules of the nations which I cast out from before you, because they do all of these, and I am disgusted by them. I have said to you: You will inherit their land, for I will give it to you as an inheritance, a land flowing with milk and honey. I am the Eternal your God who has separated you from among the peoples. You are to separate between the pure beast and the impure, and between the impure fowl and the pure. And you are not to abominate your souls with beast, with fowl, or with anything that creeps on the ground, which I have separated for you as impure. You are to be sanctified to me, for I, the Eternal, am holy. I have separated you from among the peoples to be mine. Also, a man or a woman who is sorcerer himself or a necromancer must die. Stone them. Their blood is on them.

Leviticus 20:9–27

◇ ◇ ◇

*S*peak to the priests, Aaron's sons, and say to them: He may not become impure by a corpse among his people, except for his closest relative: for his mother, for his father, for his son, for his daughter, for his brother, and for his virgin sister, closest to him, who was not with a man. He may become impure for her. As a husband, he is not to become impure among his people by profaning himself. They are not to pluck a bald-spot on their head or shave the corners of their beard or cut incisions in their flesh. They are to be sanctified to their God and not profane the name of their God, because they offer the Eternal's fire–offerings, the bread of their God. They are holy. They are not to take a soliciting or a profane woman. And they are not to take a woman divorced from her husband, because he is holy to his God. You will sanctify him, because he offers the bread of your God. He will be holy to you, for I, the Eternal your sanctifier, am holy. Therefore, the daughter of a priestly man, who profanes by soliciting, she profanes her father. She is to be burnt in fire. And the highest priest among his brothers, on whose head the anointing oil has been poured, and whose hand has been consecrated to wear the garments, should not dishevel his head and should not rend his garments. And he is not to come near any dead body. He is not to become impure for his father or for his mother. And he is not to go out of the sanctuary and not to profane the sanctuary of his God, because the crown of anointing oil of his God is on him. I am the Eternal. And he is to take a wife in her virginity. He is not to take these:

a widow, a divorcee, or a profane slut, because he is to take a virgin from his people as a wife. Therefore, he will not profane his children among his people, for I am the Eternal his sanctifier.

Leviticus 21:1–15

◇   ◇   ◇

Speak to Aaron, saying: A man of your descendants, throughout their generations, who has a deformity in him, is not to approach to offer the bread of his God. Because any man who has a deformity in him should not approach: a blind, lame, flatnosed, or elongated man; or a man who has a broken leg or a broken arm in him; or a hunchback, or a midget, or having a cataract in his eye, eczema, scurvy, or a crushed testicle. Any man of the descendants of Aaron the priest who has a deformity in him, is not to approach to offer the fire–offerings of the Eternal. While deformed, he may not approach to offer the bread of his God. He may eat the bread of his God from the holiest of holies and from the holy, but he may not come to the veil and may not approach the altar while a deformity is in him. Therefore, he will not profane my sanctuary, for I am the Eternal their sanctifier.

Leviticus 21:17–23

◇   ◇   ◇

Speak to Aaron and to his sons, that they abstain from the sanctifications of the children of Israel which they sanctify to me and not profane my holy name. I am the Eternal. Say to them: Throughout your generations, any man from among any of your descendants who approaches, while his impurity is on him, to the sanctifications which the children of Israel are to sanctify to the Eternal, that soul will be cut off from before me. I am the Eternal. Any man of the descendants of Aaron who is a leper or a discharger may not eat from the sanctifications until he is purified. And he who has touched any impure body, or who has an emission of semen, or who touches any creeper which is impure to him or a man who is impure to him, for any sort of impurity, the soul who touches it will be impure until the evening and is not to eat from the sanctifications, except if he has bathed his flesh in water. When the sun sets, he will be considered pure. And afterwards, he may eat from the sanctifications, for it is his bread. Do not eat a carcass or a mutilation, to become impure by it. I am the Eternal. Safeguard my observance, so you will not bear sin for it and die for it, by profaning it. I am the Eternal their sanctifier. No stranger may eat a sanctification. A priest's tenant and laborer may not eat a sanctification. But a priest who purchases a soul, his money-purchase, he may eat from it. Also, those born in his house may eat of his bread. But a priest's daughter who has a stranger for a husband, she may not eat of the sanctified raised—offerings. Yet, a priest's daughter who is a widow or a divorcee and does not have children, who returns to her father's house, as in her youth, she may eat of her father's bread. But no stranger may eat of it. And if a man eats a sanctification unknowingly, he is to add his fifth in excess of it and give the sanctification to the priest. Hence, they will not profane the sanctifications of the children of Israel, that which they raise for the Eternal, nor bear the guilt of iniquity when they eat the sanctifications, for I am the Eternal their sanctifier.

Leviticus 22:2–16

◇   ◇   ◇

Speak to Aaron, and to his sons, and to all the children of Israel, and say to them: Any man of the house of Israel or of the foreigners in Israel who presents his offering, for any of their vows or for any of their contributions which they would offer to the Eternal as an ascension—offering: for your acceptance, it is to be an unblemished male of the cattle, of the lambs, or of the goats. Do not offer any which has a deformity in it, because it is not to be accepted by you. Therefore, if a man offers a peace—sacrifice for the Eternal, to dedicate a vow or to contribute from the cattle or from the sheep, it must be unblemished to be accepted. It is not to have any deformity in it. Blinded, broken, maimed, warted, eczemous, scurveyed—do not offer these for the Eternal. And do not give a fire—offering of these, on the altar, for the Eternal. Also, an ox or a lamb, elongated or clubfooted, may be prepared as a contribution, but it is not to be accepted for a vow. And bruised, crushed, torn, or castrated, do not offer for the Eternal, and do not make in your land. Also, do not offer the bread of your God from any of these, from the hand of an alien, because the corruption in them is a deformity in them. They are not to be accepted by you.

Leviticus 22:18–25

◇   ◇   ◇

When an ox, a lamb, or a goat is born, it is to be under its mother for seven days. And from the eighth day on, it may be accepted as an offering, a fire—offering, for the Eternal. And an ox or a sheep—do not slaughter it and its kid on the same day. And when you sacrifice a sacrifice of thanksgiving to the Eternal, you are to sacrifice it for your acceptance. It is to be eaten on that day. Do not leave of it until morning. I am the Eternal. Safeguard my commandments and do them. I am the Eternal. And you are not to profane my holy name. I will be sanctified among the children of Israel. I am the Eternal your sanctifier who brought you out from the land of Egypt to be your God. I am the Eternal.

Leviticus 22:27–33

*S*peak to the children of Israel and say to them: The meetings of the Eternal, those which you are to call "holy callings," these are those, my meetings. You are to work for six days, but on the seventh day—a Sabbath rest, a holy calling. You are not to work at all. It is a Sabbath for the Eternal in all of your settlements. These are the meetings of the Eternal, holy callings, those which you are to proclaim in their seasons. In the first month, on the fourteenth of the month, at twilight, is the Passover for the Eternal. And on the fifteenth day of this month is the festival of unleavened bread for the Eternal. You are to eat unleavened bread for seven days. On the first day, there is to be a holy calling for you. Do not work at all. You are to offer a fire–offering for the Eternal for seven days. On the seventh day, there is to be a holy calling. Do not work at all.

Leviticus 23:2–8.

*S*peak to the children of Israel and say to them: When you come to the land which I give to you and harvest its harvest, you are to bring a sheaf of the finest of your harvest to the priest. He is to wave the sheaf before the Eternal, for your acceptance. The priest is to wave it on the morrow following the Sabbath. On the day you wave the sheaf, you are to prepare an unblemished, year-old lamb as an ascension–offering for the Eternal. And its meal–offering—two tenths flour mixed in oil, a fire–offering for the Eternal, a pleasing aroma. And its libation—a quarter gallon of wine. Do not eat bread, cornflour, or grain, until this same day, until you have brought your God's offering—an everlasting decree throughout your generations in all your settlements. And you are to count, for yourselves, from the morrow following the Sabbath, from the day you bring the sheaf for the wave–offering, seven complete weeks. Count fifty days until the morrow after the seventh week. Then, offer a new meal–offering for the

Eternal. Bring two breads as a wave–offering from your settlements. It is to be two tenths of flour. Bake it leavened, first-fruits for the Eternal. Offer seven unblemished, year-old lambs, one young bull, and two rams with the bread. They are to be an ascension–offering for the Eternal, with their meal–offering and their libation, as a fire–offering, a pleasing aroma for the Eternal. Prepare one kid goat as a sin–offering and two year-old lambs as a peace–sacrifice. The priest is to wave them with the bread of the first-fruits, and the two lambs, as a wave–offering before the Eternal. They will be sanctified to the Eternal for the priest. On this same day, you are to proclaim a holy calling for yourselves. Do not work at all—an everlasting decree in all of your settlements, throughout your generations. And when you harvest the harvest of your land, do not finish the corner of your field when you harvest. And do not glean the gleaning of your harvest. Leave them for the poor and for the stranger. I am the Eternal your God.

Leviticus 23:10–22

◇   ◇   ◇

Speak to the children of Israel, saying: In the seventh month, on the first of the month, there is to be a Sabbath for you, a memorial trumpeting, a holy calling. Do not work at all. Offer a fire–offering for the Eternal.

Leviticus 23:24–25

◇   ◇   ◇

Also, on the tenth of this seventh month, there is to be a Day of Atonement. It will be a holy calling to you. You are to humble your souls and offer a fire–offering to the Eternal. Do not work at all on this same day, because it is a Day of Atonement to atone for you before the Eternal your God. For any soul who is not humbled on this same day will be cut off from its people. And any soul who works at all on this same day, I will let that soul be lost from among its people. Do not work at all—an everlasting decree throughout your generations in all of your settlements. It is a Sabbath rest for you. Humble your souls. In the evening of the ninth of the month, from evening until evening, you must rest on your Sabbath.

Leviticus 23:27–32

◇   ◇   ◇

Speak to the children of Israel, saying: On the fifteenth day of this seventh month is the Festival of Booths, seven days for the Eternal. On the first day, there is to be a holy calling. Do not work at all. You are to offer a fire–offering for seven days, for the Eternal. On the eighth day, there is to be a holy calling for you. You are to offer a fire–offering for the Eternal. It is a convocation. Do not work at all.

Leviticus 23:34–36

*T*hese are the meetings of the Eternal, those which you are to call "holy callings," to offer a fire–offering for the Eternal, an ascension–offering, a meal–offering, a sacrifice, and libations, the daily item on its day, besides the Eternal's Sabbaths, besides your gifts, besides all of your vows, and besides all of your contributions which you give for the Eternal. Therefore, on the fifteenth day of the seventh month, when you have gathered the produce of the land, you are to celebrate the Eternal's festival for seven days. On the first day, there is to be a rest and on the eighth day, there is to be a rest. On the first day, you are to take for yourselves: fruits of the citron tree, palm branches, a bough of the myrtle tree, and willows of the brook. You are to rejoice before the Eternal your God for seven days. Celebrate it as a festival for the Eternal, seven days a year, an everlasting decree throughout your generations. Celebrate it in the seventh month. Settle in booths for seven days. Every native in Israel is to settle in booths, so that your generations will know that I settled the children of Israel in booths when I took them out from the land of Egypt. I am the Eternal your God.

Leviticus 23:37–43

*C*ommand the children of Israel to bring to you pure, pressed, olive oil for lighting, to raise a lamp, perpetually. Aaron is to arrange it outside the veil of the testimony, in the tent of meeting, from evening until morning, before the Eternal, perpetually—an everlasting decree throughout your generations. He is to arrange the lamps on the immaculate candelabrum, perpetually, before the Eternal. You are to take flour and bake it as twelve doughs, each dough having two tenths. Place them, two rows, six to the row, on the immaculate table, before the Eternal. Put fine frankincense over the row, that it be for the bread as a memorial-portion, a fire–offering for the Eternal. On every Sabbath day, he is to arrange it before the Eternal, perpetually, from the children of Israel—an everlasting contract. It will be for Aaron and for his sons. They are to eat it in a sanctified place, because it is the holiest of the holies for him from the fire–offerings of the Eternal—an everlasting decree.

Leviticus 24:2–9

*B*ring the curser outside the camp. All who hear are to lay their hands on his head, and the entire congregation is to stone him. Then, speak to the children of Israel, saying: Any man who curses his God will bear his sin. And a blasphemer of the name of the Eternal must die. The entire congregation must stone him. The foreigner, as the native, when he blasphemes the name, will die. And a man who strikes any person's life must die. And he who strikes the life of cattle will pay for it, a life for a life. And a man who deforms his colleague, as he did, so will it be done to him—a break for a break, an eye for an eye, a tooth for a tooth. Just as he causes a deformity on a man, so it will be caused on him. And he who strikes cattle will pay for it. And he who strikes a man will die. You are to have one judgment. The foreigner will be as the native, for I am the Eternal your God.

Leviticus 24:14–22

*S*peak to the children of Israel and say to them: When you come into the land which I give to you, the land is to rest a Sabbath for the Eternal. You may sow your field for six years, prune your vineyard for six years, and gather its produce, but in the seventh year the land is to have a Sabbath rest, a Sabbath for the Eternal. Do not sow your field. And do not prune your vineyard. Do not harvest the after-growth of your harvest. And do not pick your crown grapes. The land is to have a year of rest. The Sabbath of the land will be to you for food: for you, for your servants, for your maids, for your laborers, and for the settlers who live with you. For your cattle, and for the animals which are on your land, its produce will be for eating.

Leviticus25:2–7

*Y*ou are to count, for yourselves, seven Sabbath years, seven years times seven, so the days of seven Sabbath years will be forty-nine years to you. Then, let the ram's-horn blast be proclaimed in the seventh month, on the tenth of the month. On the day of Atonement, you are to let the ram's-horn be proclaimed throughout your land. You are to sanctify the fiftieth year and declare liberty in the land for all of its inhabitants. It will be a Jubilee for you. You are to restore a man's property and restore a man to his family. The fiftieth year will be your Jubilee. Do not sow, and do not harvest its after-growth. And do not pick its crowns, because it is the Jubilee. It will be sanctified for you. You may eat its produce from the field. In this Jubilee Year, you are to restore a man's property. Therefore, if you sell to your fellow-man or buy from the hand of your fellow-man, do not exploit each other. You are to buy from your fellow-man according to the number of years after the Jubilee. He is to sell to you according to the number of years of produce. You are to multiply its price according to the multiple of years and decrease its price according to the fewness of years, for he sells you a sum of produce. Thus, a man is not to exploit his fellow-man but is to fear your God, for I am the Eternal your God. Fulfill my decrees and observe my judgments, and do them. Settle the land in security. The land will bear its fruits. You will eat until satiety and settle over it in security. And yet you say: "What will we eat in the seventh year, if we do not sow and do not reap our produce?" I will command my blessing upon you in the sixth year and provide for the three years. You are to sow in the eighth year and eat of the old produce until the ninth year. You are to eat of the old until produce comes. Also, you may not sell the land permanently, because the land is mine—because you are foreigners and settlers with me. Therefore, in the entire land of your property, you are to give redemption to the land.

Leviticus 25:8–24

◇   ◇   ◇

*I*f your brother becomes impoverished and sells his property, his closest redeemer should come to him (the purchaser) and redeem his brother's sale. And a man who does not have a redeemer, but his hand affords it and finds enough for its redemption, is to consider the years of his sale, restore the surplus to the man to whom he sold, and return to his property. But if his hand cannot find enough restoration for him, his sale is to be in the hand of its buyer until the Jubilee Year. It will go out in the Jubilee, and he will return to his property.

Leviticus 25:25–28

And if a man sells a residential house in a walled city, its redemption may be until the completion of the year of its sale. You are to have its redemption for a year. But if it is not redeemed until the culmination of a complete year, the house which is in the city which has a wall is permanently established for its buyer, for his generations. It will not go out in the Jubilee. But the houses of the villages which do not have a surrounding wall are to be considered as the fields of the land. They will have redemption and go out in the Jubilee. And the cities of the Levites, the houses of the cities of their property—an everlasting redemption will be for the Levites, even when redeemed from the Levites. Therefore, a sale of a house or city of his property will go out in the Jubilee, because the houses of the cities of the Levites are their property among the children of Israel. Therefore, the field-lots of their cities are not to be sold, because it is their everlasting property.

Leviticus 25:29–34

◇   ◇   ◇

And if your brother becomes impoverished and his hand is lowered to you, you are to strengthen him, a foreigner or a resident, so he may live with you. Do not take interest or charges from him, but fear your God, so your brother may live with you. Do not give him your money with interest. And do not give your food for charges. I am the Eternal your God who brought you out from the land of Egypt to give you the land of Canaan, to be your God. And if your brother becomes impoverished with you and is sold to you, do not let him serve the service of a slave. He is to be with you as a laborer, as a settler. He is to serve with you until the Jubilee Year and will go out from you, he and his sons with him, and return to his family. Therefore, he is to be restored to the portion of his fathers, for they are my servants, those whom I have brought out from the land of Egypt. They are not to be sold at a slave–sale. Do not rule over him oppressively, but fear your God. Therefore, your servant and your maid whom you will have will be from the nations around you. You may buy a servant and a maid from them and also from the children of the settlers who live among you. You may buy from them and from their families who are with you, who were born in your land. They are to be to you as property. You may possess them for your children after you as inherited property. You may be served by them forever. But as for your brothers, the children of Israel, one over the next, do not rule over him oppressively. And if a foreigner or a settler with you becomes wealthy, but your brother with him becomes poor and is sold to the foreign settler with you or to an offspring of the foreigner's family: after he is sold, he is to have redemption. One of his brothers is to redeem him. Either his uncle or his cousin is to redeem him. Or he may be redeemed by a relative of his flesh, by his family. Or if he can afford it, so will he be redeemed. He will consider with his buyer, from the year of his sale to him until the Jubilee Year. The money of his sale is to be according to the number of years. As the days of a laborer, it is to be with him. If it be many years more, according to them, he is to restore his redemption, for the money of his purchase. And if few years remain until the Jubilee Year, it is to be considered for him. According to his years, he is to restore his redemption. He is to be with him as a laborer, year by year. In your eyes, he may not rule over him oppressively. And if he is not redeemed by these, he is to go out in the Jubilee Year, he and his children with him, for the children of Israel are servants to me. They are my servants whom I brought out from the land of Egypt. I am the Eternal your God.

Leviticus 25:35–55

◇ ◇ ◇

*D*o not make idols for yourselves. And do not erect a monument or a statue for yourselves. And do not put a stone mosaic in your land for bowing over it, for I am the Eternal your God. Safeguard my Sabbaths, and fear my sanctuary. I am the Eternal.

Leviticus 26:1–2

◇ ◇ ◇

*I*f you follow my decrees, safeguard my commandments, and do them, I will give your rains in their times, the land will bear its crop, and the tree of the field will bear its fruit. For you, threshing will reach until vintage, and vintage will reach until sowing. You will eat your bread until satiety and settle securely in your land. I will give peace in the land, so you may relax and not be frightened. I will remove evil animals from the land, and a sword will not pass through your land. You will chase your enemies, and they will fall before you by the sword. Five of you will chase a hundred, and a hundred of you will chase ten thousand. Your enemies will fall before you by the sword. I will turn to you and make you fruitful, multiply you, and establish my contract with you. You could eat the old obsolete, but you will take out the old because of the new. I will put my tabernacle among you, so my soul will not loathe you. And I, myself, will go among you. I will be your God, and you will be my people. I am the Eternal your God who brought you out from the land of Egypt, from being servants to them. I have broken the bars of your yoke and have made you walk upright.

Leviticus 26:3–13

*B*ut if you will not listen to me and will not do all of these commandments, if you despise my decrees, and if your soul loathes my judgments, therefore not doing any of my commandments, annulling my contract, I too will do this to you. I will punish you with confusion, with consumption, and with fever consuming the eyes and grieving the soul. You will sow your seed in vain, and your enemies will eat it. I will oppose you. You will be stricken before your enemies. Your foes will rule over you, and you will flee although you are not chased. And if thus far, you do not listen to me, I will continue to chastise you sevenfold for your sins. I will break the glory of your strength. I will make your heavens as iron and your land as copper. You will exhaust your power in vain. And your land will not bear its crop. And the tree of the land will not bear its fruit. Then, if you go adversely with me and do not come to listen to me, I will add a blow upon you sevenfold as your sins. I will send the animals of the field on you, bereave you, destroy your cattle, and reduce you. Your roads will be desolate. Then, if you are not chastised for me by these, and you go adversely with me, so also I will go adversely with you. Again, I will strike you sevenfold for your sins. I will bring an avenging sword on you, avenging my contract. You will be gathered into your cities, and I will send an epidemic among you. You will be given into the hand of the enemy. When the staff of bread is broken for you, ten women will bake your bread in one oven and return your bread by weight. You will eat but not be satisfied. And if with these, you do not listen to me and go adversely with me, I will go adversely with you in anger, and again I will chastise you sevenfold for your sins. You will eat the flesh of your sons, and you will eat the flesh of your daughters. I will demolish your pulpits, destroy your sun-gods, and put your corpses on the corpses of your idols. My soul will despise you. I will give your cities to ruin and devastate your sanctuaries; and I will not smell your pleasing aromas. I will devastate the land, and your enemies who settle in it will be devastating upon it. And I will scatter you among the nations and draw a sword after you. Your land will become desolate, and your cities will be ruined. Then the land will be contented by her Sabbaths. All the days of its desolation, while you are in the land of your enemies, then the land will rest and be contented by her Sabbaths. All the days of its desolation, it will rest because it did not rest in your Sabbaths, when you settled on it. And the remainder of you, I will bring cowardice into their hearts, in the land of their enemies. The sound of a falling leaf will chase them. They will flee as though fleeing from a sword, and they will fall, although none chase. They will stumble, one over the next, as before a sword, although none chase. And you will not resist your enemies. You will be lost among the nations. The land of your enemies will devour you. And the remainder of you will rot in their sin in the lands of your enemies. And they will rot, also, with the sins of their fathers on them. They will confess their sin and the sin of their fathers in their transgression which they committed against me, and also that they went adversely with me, so I went adversely with them and brought them into their enemies' land. Maybe then, they will submit their uncircumcised hearts. And then, they will be sufficed with their sin. I will remember my contract with Jacob, and also my contract with Isaac, and also I will remember my contract with Abraham; and I will remember the land. Hence, the land will be abandoned by them but will be contented with its Sabbaths in its desolation from them. And they will be sufficed with their sin, because they abhorred my judgments, and because their soul despised my decrees. Yet, also even this: while they are in their enemies' land, they will not be hated and will not be despised to their extinction, to annul my contract with them, for I am the Eternal their God. I will remember, for them, the contract of the first-ones, those whom I brought out from the land of Egypt before the eyes of the nations to be their God. I am the Eternal.

Leviticus 26:14–45

◇   ◇   ◇

*S*peak to the children of Israel and say to them: When a man proclaims a vow for the Eternal, let it be according your assessment of beings. For your assessment of the male from twenty years old and until sixty years old, your assessment will be fifty shekels of silver of the holy shekel. And if she is female, your assessment will be thirty shekels. And if from five years old until twenty years old, your assessment of the male will be twenty shekels and for the female, ten shekels. And if from a month old until five years old, your assessment of the male will be five shekels of silver, and for the female your assessment is three shekels of silver. And if from sixty years old and above: If male, your assessment will be fifteen shekels, and for the female—ten shekels. But if he becomes poor from your assessment, he is to present himself to the priest, and the priest is to assess him. The priest is to assess him according to what he who vows can afford. And if it is a beast from which they may offer an offering for the Eternal, all given from it for the Eternal will be sanctified. He is not to convert it and may not exchange it—good for bad, or bad for good. And if he exchanges a beast for a beast, it and its exchange will be sanctified. And if it is any impure beast from which they are not to offer an offering for the Eternal, he will present the beast to the priest, and the priest is to assess it—whether good or bad. It is to be according to your priest's assessment. But if he would redeem it, he is to add its fifth beyond your assessment.

Leviticus 27:2–13

And when a man dedicates his house to be holy for the Eternal, the priest is to assess it—whether good or bad. As the priest assesses it, so it is to be established. But if the dedicator would redeem his house, he is to add its fifth of silver beyond your assessment of it, and it will be his.

Leviticus 27:14–15

And if a man dedicates the field of his property for the Eternal, your assessment is to be according to its seed: a heap of barley seed for fifty shekels of silver. If he dedicates his field from the Jubilee Year, it is to be established by your assessment. And if he dedicates his field after the Jubilee, the priest is to consider the silver for him according to the years remaining until the Jubilee Year and deduct from your assessment. But if its dedicator would redeem the field, he is to add its fifth of silver beyond your assessment, and it will be established for him. And if he does not redeem the field but sells the field to another man, it may not be redeemed further. When the field goes out in the Jubilee, it will be sanctified for the Eternal, as the forfeited field. It will be the priest's property. Yet, if he dedicated his purchased field which is not from the field of his property, for the Eternal, the priest is to consider for him the amount of your assessment until the Jubilee Year and give your assessment on that day, a sanctification for the Eternal. In the Jubilee Year, the field is to return to whomever he purchased it from, to whomever the property of the land belongs. And all of your assessing is to be in the holy shekel. The shekel is to be twenty pennyweights.

Leviticus 27:16–25

And a firstborn of the cattle which is a firstborn for the Eternal, no one is to dedicate. Whether ox or lamb, it is for the Eternal. But if it is from the impure cattle, it may be ransomed according to your assessment. He is to add its fifth in excess of it. And if it is not redeemed, it is to be sold according to your assessment. And any forfeit which a man forfeits for the Eternal from all that is his—man, beast, or field of his property—may not be sold and may not be redeemed. All forfeit is the holiest of holies for the Eternal. Any forfeit which he forfeits from man may not be ransomed. He must die. And any tithe of the land, of the seed of the land or of the fruit of the tree, is for the Eternal, a sanctification for the Eternal. But if a man would redeem of his tithes, he is to add its fifth in excess of it. And any tithe of bull or sheep, all which passes under the rod, the tenth is to be sanctified for the Eternal. Do not examine whether it is good or bad. And do not exchange them. Because if you exchange them, it and its exchange will be sanctified. It is not to be redeemed.

Leviticus 27:26–33

NUMBERS

*T*ake the census of the entire congregation of the children of Israel by their families, by the house of their fathers, by the number of names, every male by their poll-tax, from twenty years old and above, all who go out in the army of Israel. You and Aaron are to number them by their armies, and a man is to be with you for each tribe. He is to be the head man for the house of his fathers. And these are the names of the men who are to stand with you: for Reuben, Elizur, son of Shedeur; for Simeon, Shelumiel, son of Zurishaddai; for Judah, Nachshon, son of Amminadab; for Issachar, Nathanel, son of Zuar; for Zebulun, Eliab, son of Chelon; for the children of Joseph: for Ephraim, Elishama, son of Amihud: for Menashe, Gamliel, son of Pedahzur; for Benjamin, Abidan, son of Gidoni; for Dan, Achiezer, son of Ammishaddai; for Asher, Pagiel, son of Ocran; for Gad, Eliasaph, son of Deuel; for Naphtali, Achira, son of Enan.

Numbers 1:2–15

*B*ut do not number the tribe of Levi, and do not take their census among the children of Israel. Hence, you are to appoint the Levites over the tabernacle of the testimony, over all of its utensils, and over all belonging to it. They are to bear the tabernacle and all of its utensils, and they are to officiate for it. Therefore, they are to encamp around the tabernacle. And when the tabernacle travels, the Levites are to take it down. And when the tabernacle is encamped, the Levites are to establish it.

And the stranger who approaches will die. The children of Israel are to encamp, each man by his camp and each man by his flag, throughout their armies. But the Levites are to encamp around the tabernacle of the testimony, so (God's) anger will not be on the congregation of the children of Israel. The Levites are to safeguard the observance of the tabernacle of testimony.

Numbers 1:49–53

◇　◇　◇

The children of Israel are to encamp, each man by his flag, by the sign of his father's house. They are to encamp afar around the tent of meeting. And the campers eastwards, in front—the flag of the camp of Judah, by its armies. And the leader of the sons of Judah, Nachshon, son of Amminadab. And his army and its numbers—seventy-four thousand and six hundred. And the campers with him—the tribe of Issachar. And the leader of the sons of Issachar, Nathanel, son of Zuar. And his army and his numbers—fifty-four thousand and four hundred. For the tribe of Zebulun: the leader of the sons of Zebulun, Eliab, son of Chelon. And his army and his numbers—fifty-seven thousand and four hundred. All of the numbered of the camp of Judah—a hundred and eighty-six thousand and four hundred, by its armies. They will travel first. Southwards, for the flag of the camp of Reuben, by its armies: the leader of the sons of Reuben, Elizur, son of Shedeur. And his army and his numbers—forty-six thousand and five hundred. And the campers with him—for the tribe of Simeon: the leader of the sons of Simeon, Shelumiel, son of Zurishaddai. And his army and its numbers—fifty-nine thousand and three hundred. And for the tribe of Gad: the leader of the sons of Gad, Eliasaph, son of Reuel. And his army and its numbers—forty-five thousand and six hundred and fifty. All the numbered of the camp of Reuben—a hundred and fifty-one thousand and four hundred and fifty, by its armies. And they will travel second. The tent of meeting, the camp of the Levites, is to travel among the camps. Just as they encamp, so are they to travel, each man with his hand by his flag. ·Westwards, for the flag of the camp of Ephraim by his armies: the leader of the sons of Ephraim, Elishama, son of Amihud. And his army and its numbers—forty thousand and five hundred. And with him, for the tribe of Menashe: the leader of the sons of Menashe, Gamliel, son of Pedahzur. And his army and its numbers—thirty-two thousand and two hundred. And for the tribe of Benjamin: the leader of the sons of Benjamin, Abidan, son of Gidoni. And his army and its numbers—thirty-five thousand and four hundred. All the numbered of the tribe of Ephraim—a hundred and eight thousand and a hundred, by its armies. And they will travel third. Northwards, for the flag of the camp of Dan by its armies: the leader of the sons of Dan, Achiezer, son of Ammishaddai. And his army and its numbers—sixty-two thousand and seven hundred. And the campers with him, for the camp of Asher: the leader of the sons of Asher, Pagiel, son of Ocran. And his army and its numbers—forty-one thousand and five hundred. And for the tribe of Naphtali: the leader of the sons of Naphtali, Achira, son of Enan. And his army and its numbers—fifty-three thousand and four hundred. All the numbered of the camp of Dan—a hundred and fifty-seven thousand and six hundred. They will travel afterwards, by their flags.

Numbers 2:2–31

*L*et the tribe members of Levi approach and stand before Aaron the priest, so they may officiate with him. They are to safeguard his observance and the observance of all the congregation before the tent of meeting, to serve the service of the tabernacle. They are to safeguard all of the utensils of the tent of meeting and the charge of the children of Israel, to serve the service of the tabernacle. You are to give the Levites to Aaron and to his sons. They must be given to him from among the children of Israel. Therefore, you are to order Aaron and his sons to safeguard their priesthood. The stranger who approaches will die.

Numbers 3:6–10

*A*nd here, I have taken the Levites from among the children of Israel instead of every firstborn who opens a womb among the children of Israel. The Levites are mine, because every firstborn is mine. On the day I struck every firstborn in the land of Egypt, I sanctified for myself every firstborn in Israel, from man until beast. They will be mine. I am the Eternal.

Numbers 3:12–13

*N*umber the children of Levi by the house of their fathers, by their families. Number them, every male, from a month old and upward.

Numbers 3:15

*N*umber every firstborn male among the children of Israel from a month old and upward, and take the count of their names. Take the Levites for me—I am the Eternal—instead of every firstborn among the children of Israel, and the cattle of the Levites instead of every firstborn among the cattle of the children of Israel.

Numbers 3:40–41

*T*ake the Levites instead of every firstborn among the children of Israel and the cattle of the Levites instead of their cattle. The Levites will be mine. I am the Eternal. And for the two hundred and seventy-three redemptions, the surplus over the Levites among the firstborn of the children of Israel, take five shekels each as a poll-tax. Take it in the holy shekel: twenty pennyweights is the shekel. Give the silver to Aaron and to his sons as redemptions for their surplus.

Numbers 3:45–48

*T*ake the census of the sons of Kehath from among the children of Levi by their families, by the house of their fathers, from thirty years old and upward, until fifty years old, all coming to the army, to do work in the tent of meeting. This is the service of the sons of Kehath in the tent of meeting: the holiest of the holies. When the camp travels, Aaron and his sons are to come. They are to take down the screening veil and cover the ark of the testimony with it. They are to put the lambskin covering over it, spread a complete blue cloth above it, and set its poles. Then, they are to spread a blue cloth over the display table and put the dishes, the spoons, the racks, and the supports of the screen on it, and the perpetual bread–offering is to be on it. They are to spread scarlet-crimson cloth over them, cover it with a lambskin covering, and set its poles. They are to take a blue cloth and cover the candelabrum of light, its lamps, its tongs, its ash-pans, and all of its oil utensils, those with which they officiate. They are to put it and all its utensils into a lambskin covering and set it on the rod. Then they are to spread a blue cloth over the golden altar, cover it with a lambskin covering, and set its poles. They are to take all of the officiating utensils, those with which they officiate in the sanctuary, put them into a blue cloth, cover them with a lambskin covering, and set them on the rod. They are to remove the ashes from the altar, spread a purple cloth over it, and put all of its utensils on it, those with which they officiate: the ash-pans, the forks, the shovels, and the basins—all the utensils of the altar. They are to spread a lambskin covering over it, and set its poles. When Aaron and his sons finish covering the sanctuary and all of the utensils of the sanctuary, and the camp travels, then afterwards, the sons of Kehath are to come and carry it. Thereby, they will not touch the sanctuary and die. This is the burden of the sons of Kehath in the tent of meeting. And the charge of Eleazar, the son of Aaron the priest: oil for the light, the incense of spices, the perpetual offering, the anointing oil, the charge of the entire tabernacle and all that is in it, in the sanctuary and in its vessels.

Numbers 4:2–16

Do not cut off the tribe of the family of the Kehathites from among the Levites. But do this to them, so they live and not die when they approach the holiest of holies. Aaron and his sons are to come and place them, each man at his service and at his burden: that they not come to see the enwrapping of the sanctuary and die.

Numbers 4:18–20

Take the census of the sons of Gershon by the house of their fathers, by their families. Number them from thirty years old and upward, until fifty years old, all who come to arm the army, to serve the service in the tent of meeting. This is the service of the family of the Gershonites, to serve and to be burdened. They are to bear the curtains of the tabernacle and the tent of meeting, its coverings, the lambskin covering which is over it, above, the screen of the entrance to the tent of meeting, the hangings of the enclosure, the screen of the entrance to the gate of the enclosure which is by the tabernacle and around by the altar, their chords, all of the utensils of their service, and all that is made for them—they are to serve. All of the service of the sons of the Gershonites, for all their burdens and for all their service is to be according to Aaron and his sons. You are to charge them with the observance of all of their burdens. This is the service of the family of the sons of the Gershonites in the tent of meeting and their observance at the hand of Ithamar, son of Aaron the priest.

Numbers 4:22–28

*Y*ou will number them, the sons of Merari, by their families, by the house of their fathers. Number them from thirty years old and upward, until fifty years old, all who come to the army, to serve the service of the tent of meeting. And this is the observance of their burden for all of their service in the tent of meeting: the boards of the tabernacle, its latches, its posts, its sockets, the posts of the surrounding enclosure, their sockets, their pegs, and their chords, for all of their utensils and for all of their service. And you are to appoint them by name for the utensils, for the observance of their burden. This is the service of the family of the sons of Merari, for all of their service in the tent of meeting, at the hand of Ithamar, son of Aaron the priest.

Numbers 4:29–33

*C*ommand the children of Israel to send every leper, every discharger, and all impure of soul from the camp. Send them whether male or female. Send them outside the camp. Thereby, they will not defile their camps in which I dwell.

Numbers 5:2–3

*S*ay to the children of Israel: When a man or a woman does any of the sins of man, committing a transgression against the Eternal, and that person is guilty, he is to confess his sin which he has committed, amend for his guilt in its principal, add its fifth in excess of it, and give it to whom he is guilty toward. But if a man does not have a redeemer to restore the guilt-causing thing to, the guilt-causing thing is to be restored to the Eternal, to the priest, besides the ram of the atonements with which he is to be atoned for. Therefore, any raised-offering for any of the sanctifications of the children of Israel which they offer to the priest is to be his (the priest's). And each man's sanctifications are to be his (the priest's). A man who gives to the priest—it (the sanctified offering) is to be his (the priest's).

Numbers 5:6–10

*S*peak to the children of Israel and say to them: If any man's wife deviates and commits a transgression against him, and a man lies with her, with seminal emission, and it is hidden from the eyes of her husband, and it is secret, but she becomes impure, and there is no witness against her, and she was not forced, and the spirit of jealousy passes over him, and he is jealous of his wife, and she is impure, or the spirit of jealousy passes over him, and he is jealous of his wife, yet she has not become impure, the man is to bring his wife to the priest and bring her offering with her: a tenth of a bushel of barley flour, no oil poured on it and no frankincense put on it, for it is a meal–offering of jealousy, a memorial meal–offering, a remembrance of guilt. The priest is to let her approach and stand before the Eternal. The priest is to take sanctified water in a clay vessel, and the priest is to take of the dust which is on the ground of the tabernacle and put it into the water. The priest is to stand the woman before the Eternal, dishevel the woman's head, and put the memorial meal–offering over her palms. It is the meal–offering of jealousy. And the bitter waters which curse are to be in the hand of the priest. The priest is to entreat her and say to the woman, "If a man did not lie with you, and if you have not deviated impurely behind your husband's back, be free from these bitter waters which curse. But if you have deviated behind your husband's back, and if you are impure, and a man besides your husband has put his bedding over you . . . ," the priest is to entreat the woman with the oath of swearing. The priest is to say to the woman, ". . . the Eternal will put you to a swearing and to an oath among your people when the Eternal makes your thigh fallen and your belly swollen. These waters which curse will enter your intestines to swell the belly and to make the thigh fall." The woman is to say: "Amen! Amen!" The priest is to write these oaths in a book and blot it with the bitter waters. The woman is to drink the bitter waters which curse. The waters which curse will come into her for bitterness. The priest is to take the meal–offering of jealousy from the woman's hand, wave the meal–offering before the Eternal, and offer it on the altar. The priest is to scoop its memorial-portion from the meal–offering and incinerate it on the altar. And afterwards, the woman is to drink the water. The water will be drunk. It will be, if she is impure and she has committed a transgression against her husband, the waters which curse will come into her for bitterness. Her belly will swell, her thigh will fall, and the woman will be forsworn among her people. But if the woman has not become impure, she is pure. She is innocent and will conceive children. This is the law of jealousies when a wife deviates behind her husband's back and becomes impure, or for a man when the spirit of jealousy passes over him and he is jealous of his wife. He is to stand the wife before the Eternal. The priest is to prepare all of the law for her. The man will be innocent from sin, but his woman will bear her sin.

Numbers 5:12–31

Speak to the children of Israel and say to them: If a man or a woman proclaims to make a vow of abstention, to abstain for the Eternal, he is to abstain from wine and from liquor. He is not to drink a fermentation of wine or a fermentation of liquor. And he is not to drink any tincture of grapes. And he is not to eat fresh or dried grapes. All the days of his abstinence, he is not to eat from all which is made from the grapevine, from the kernels to the husk. All the days of his vow of abstinence, a razor may not pass over his head. Until the days which he is abstaining for the Eternal are culminated, he is to be sanctified, the hair of his head growing disheveled. All the days of his abstinence for the Eternal, he is not to come across a dead body. For his father and for his mother, for his brother and for his sister, he is not to become impure for them when they die, because the crown of his God is on his head. All the days of his abstinence, he is sanctified for the Eternal. If a man dies by him with sudden unexpectedness, and the crown of his head becomes impure, he is to shave his head on the day of his purification. He is to shave it on the seventh day. And on the eighth day, he is to bring two doves or two young pigeons to the priest by the entrance of the tent of meeting. The priest is to prepare one as a sin–offering and one as an ascension–offering and atone for him, for what he has sinned on account of the body. He is to sanctify his head on that day. He is to consecrate the days of his abstinence for the Eternal and bring a year-old lamb as a guilt–offering. But the first days are to be omitted, because his abstinence was impure.

Numbers 6:2–12

◊   ◊   ◊

And this is the law of the abstainer on the day of his culmination of the days of his abstention. He is to be brought to the entrance of the tent of meeting. He is to present his offering for the Eternal: one unblemished year-old lamb for an ascension–offering, one unblemished year-old ewe for a sin–offering, one unblemished ram for a peace–offering, a basket of unleavened doughs of flour mixed in oil, unleavened wafers anointed in oil, their meal–offerings, and their libations. The priest is to offer it before the Eternal and prepare his sin–offering and his ascension–offering. And he is to prepare the ram, a peace–sacrifice for the Eternal, in addition to the basket of unleavened breads. The priest is to prepare his meal–offering and his libation. The abstainer is to shave the crown of his head by the entrance of the tent of meeting, take the hair of the crown of his head, and put it on the fire which is under the peace–sacrifice. The priest is to take the boiled shoulder of the ram, and one unleavened dough from the basket, one unleavened wafer, and put it over the palms of the abstainer, after he has shaved his crown. The priest is to wave them, a wave–offering before the Eternal. It is sanctified for the priest as the breast of the wave–offering and as the shank of the raised–offering. Then afterwards, the abstainer may drink wine. This is the law of the abstainer who vows his offering to the Eternal for his abstention, according to what he can afford. According to his vow which he has made, so will he do in addition to the law of his abstention.

Numbers 6:13–21

Speak to Aaron and to his sons, saying: Thus bless the children of Israel, saying to them: May the Eternal bless you and guard you. May the Eternal shine his face upon you and be gracious to you. May the Eternal lift his face to you and make peace for you. They are to place my name over the children of Israel, and I will bless them.

Numbers 6:23–27

Take from them. They are to perform the service of the tent of meeting. Give them to the Levites, each man according to his service.

Numbers 7:5

One leader a day, one leader each day, is to present his offering for the inauguration of the altar.

Numbers 7:11

Speak to Aaron and say to him: When you raise the lamps, the seven lamps are to shine across the face of the candelabrum.

Numbers 8:2

Take the Levites from among the children of Israel and purify them. And, thus do to them, to purify them: splash the water of the sin–offering over them. They are to pass a razor over all of their skin, wash their clothes, and purify themselves. They are to take a young bull and its meal–offering, flour mixed in oil, and you are to take a second young bull as a sin–offering. Let the Levites approach before the tent of meeting. Assemble the entire congregation of the children of Israel. Let the Levites approach before the Eternal. The children of Israel are to lay their hands on the Levites. Aaron is to wave the Levites—a wave–offering before the Eternal from the children of Israel. They are to perform the service of the Eternal. Then, the Levites are to lay their hands on the head of the bulls, and one is to be prepared as a sin–offering and one as an ascension–offering for the Eternal, to atone for the Levites. Stand the Levites before Aaron and before his sons and wave them—a wave–offering for the Eternal. Separate the Levites from among the children of Israel. The Levites will be mine. Afterwards, the Levites are to come to serve the tent of meeting. Purify them and wave them as a wave–offering, because they must be given to me from among the children of Israel. I have taken them for myself instead of the firstling of every womb, every firstborn among the children of Israel, because every firstborn among the children of Israel, man or beast, is mine. I sanctified them for myself on the day I struck every firstborn in the land of Egypt. I have taken the Levites instead of every firstborn of the children of Israel. Indeed, I have given the Levites to Aaron and to his sons from among the children of Israel, to perform the service of the children of Israel in the tent of meeting and to atone for the children of Israel, so the children of Israel will not be plagued when the children of Israel approach the sanctuary.

Numbers 8:6–19

This is what is for the Levites. From twenty-five years old and upward, he is to come to enlist in the army of the service of the tent of meeting. And from fifty years old, he is to return from the army of service and perform no more. He is to officiate for his brothers in the tent of meeting, to safeguard the observance. But he is not to perform the service. This you are to do for the Levites in their observance.

Numbers 8:24–26

The children of Israel are to prepare the Passover–offering in its season. You are to prepare it on the fourteenth day in this month (Aviv—the month of Spring), at twilight, in its season. You are to prepare it by all of its laws and by all of its judgments.

Numbers 9:2–3

*S*peak to the children of Israel, saying: If any man is rendered impure by a corpse or is on a faraway road, for you or for your generations, and would prepare the Passover–offering for the Eternal, he is to prepare it in the second month, on the fourteenth day, at twilight. He is to eat it with unleavened bread and bitter herbs. He may not leave of it until morning, and he may not break a bone in it. He is to prepare it by all the laws of the Passover–offering. But the man who is pure and not on the road, who refrains from preparing the Passover–offering, that soul will be cut off from among his people, because he did not offer the Eternal's offering in its season. That man will bear his sin. And if a foreigner lives with you and prepares a Passover–offering for the Eternal, he is to prepare it by the laws of the Passover–offering and by its judgments. There is to be one law for you, for the foreigner and the native of the land.

Numbers 9:10–14

◇ ◇ ◇

*M*ake yourself two silver trumpets. Make them beaten. They are to be for you, for calling the congregation and for the traveling of the camps. Blow with them, and the entire congregation will gather to you by the entrance of the tent of meeting. But if they (the priests) blow with one (trumpet), the leaders, the heads of the thousands of Israel, are to meet with you. Blow a blast, and the camps which have encamped eastward are to travel. Blow a second blast, the camps which have encamped southward are to travel. They are to blow a blast for their traveling. And when the assembly gathers, you are to blow, but you are not to blast. Therefore, the sons of Aaron the priest are to blow with the trumpets. It will be to you as an everlasting decree throughout their generations. And if a war comes to your land with the enemy who oppresses you, you are to blow with the trumpets. You will be remembered before the Eternal your God and saved from your enemies. And on the day of your rejoicing, at your meetings, and at the beginnings of your months, you are to blow with the trumpets over your ascension–offerings and over your peace–sacrifices. They will be to you as a memorial before your God. I am the Eternal your God.

Numbers 10:2–10

◇ ◇ ◇

*G*ather me seventy men of the elders of Israel, those who you know are elders of the people and their executives. Take them to the tent of meeting. They are to be stationed there with you. I will descend and

speak with you there. I will impart from the spirit which is on you and put
it on them (the elders). They are to bear with you in the burden of the
people, so you will not bear it alone. Therefore, you are to say to the
people: Sanctify yourselves for tomorrow. You are to eat meat, because you
have cried in the ears of the Eternal, saying: "Who will feed us meat? It was
good for us in Egypt." The Eternal will give you meat. You will eat. You will
eat not one day, nor two days, nor five days, nor ten days, nor twenty
days—but up to a month of days, until it comes out your nose and is
repulsive to you, because you have despised the Eternal who is in your
midst. You have cried before him, saying, "Why did we leave Egypt for
this?"

Numbers 11:16–20

*I*s the Eternal short-handed? Now you will see whether or not my
word will happen to you.

Numbers 11:23

*Y*ou three, go out to the tent of meeting.

Numbers 12:4

*N*ow hear my words: If you will have a prophet, I, the Eternal,
will become known to him in a vision. I will speak to him in a dream. Not
so my servant Moses. Among my whole house, he is faithful. I will speak
with him mouth to mouth, with vision, and not in riddles; and he will view
the image of the Eternal. Therefore, why were you not afraid to speak
against my servant, against Moses?

Numbers 12:6–8

*I*f her father must spit in her face, should she not be ashamed for
seven days? Shut her outside the camp for seven days. Afterwards, collect
her.

Numbers 12:14

*S*end men for yourself. They are to explore the land of Canaan which I give to the children of Israel. Send one man for each tribe of his fathers, each of them a leader.

Numbers 13:2

*H*ow long will this people despise me? And how long will they not believe in me, in all of the signs which I made among them? I will strike them with an epidemic and dispossess them. I will make you into a larger and mightier nation than they.

Numbers 14:11–12

I have forgiven according to your word. But, nevertheless, as I am living and the glory of the Eternal fills all of the earth, since all the men who have seen my glory and my signs, which I have made in Egypt and in the desert, have tested me these ten times and have not listened to my voice, they will not see the land which I have sworn to their fathers. And all who despise me will not see it. But my servant Caleb, because he had another spirit with him and is consecrated to me, I will bring him to the land, there where he came, and his descendants will inherit it. Yet, the Amalekites and the Canaanites are settled in the valley. Tomorrow, turn and travel, for yourselves, to the desert, the Red Sea route.

Numbers 14:20–25

*H*ow long will this evil congregation complain against me? I have heard the complaints of the children of Israel which they have made against me. Say to them: As I live, declares the Eternal, as you have spoken in my ears, so will I do to you. Your corpses and all of your numbered by all of your countings, from twenty years old and upward, who have complained against me will fall in this desert. You will not enter the land which I have lifted my hand for you to dwell in, except for Caleb, son of Jephunneh, and Joshua, son of Nun. But your children who you said would be for prey, them I will bring in. They will know the land which you have despised. But you, your corpses will fall in this desert. Therefore, your children will wander in the desert for forty years. They will bear your solicitousness until your corpses are finished in the desert. For the number of days that you explored the land, forty days, a year for each day you will bear your iniquity; forty years you will know my opposition. I, the Eternal, have spoken. I will do this to all of this evil congregation who meet against me. They will be finished in this desert, and they will die there.

Numbers 14:27–35

◇ ◇ ◇

*S*peak to the children of Israel and say to them: When you come to the land of your settlements which I give you, and you prepare a fire–offering for the Eternal, an ascension–offering, or a sacrifice to proclaim a vow, or a contribution, or at your festivals, to prepare a pleasing aroma for the Eternal from the cattle or from the sheep, the offerer will prepare his offering for the Eternal—a meal–offering, a tenth of flour mixed with a quarter gallon of oil. And you are to prepare a quarter gallon of wine for a libation over the ascension–offering or for the sacrifice. For each lamb or ram, you are to prepare a meal–offering—two tenths of flour mixed with a third of a gallon of wine. And you are to prepare wine for the libation, a third of a gallon, a pleasing aroma for the Eternal. And when you prepare a young bull, an ascension–offering, or a sacrifice to proclaim a vow, or peace–offerings for the Eternal, offer a meal–offering in addition to the young bull—three tenths of flour mixed in half a gallon of oil. And offer half a gallon of wine for a libation, a fire–offering, a pleasing aroma for the Eternal. Thus will be done for each ox, for each ram, and for the lamb of the sheep or of the goats. By the number that you prepare, so are you to prepare each one, accordingly. Every native is to prepare these, as such, to offer a fire–offering, a pleasing aroma for the Eternal. And if a foreigner lives with you or is among you for your generations, and he is to prepare a fire–offering, a pleasing aroma for the Eternal, as you do, so will he do. For the assembly: one decree for you and for the residing stranger—an everlasting decree throughout your generations. The foreigner is to be like you before the Eternal. One law, one judgment, is to be for you and for the foreigner who lives among you.

Numbers 15:2–16

*S*peak to the children of Israel and say to them: When you come to the land where I am bringing you and you eat from the bread of the land, you are to raise a raised–offering for the Eternal. You are to raise the first of your rolls of dough as a raised–offering. As the raised–offering of the mill, so are you to raise it. You are to give of the first of your rolls for the Eternal, a raised–offering throughout your generations.

Numbers 15:18–21

*A*nd if you err and do not do all of these commandments which the Eternal has told to Moses, all that the Eternal has commanded you by the hand of Moses from the day that the Eternal commanded you and henceforth throughout your generations: it will be, if it was done in ignorance in the eyes of the congregation, the entire congregation is to prepare one young bull as an ascension–offering, as a pleasing aroma for the Eternal, its meal–offering and its oblation, as customary; and one kid goat as a sin–offering. The priest is to atone for the entire congregation of the children of Israel, and they will be forgiven, because it is ignorance. Therefore, they are to bring their offering, a fire–offering for the Eternal, and their sin–offering before the Eternal, for their ignorance. The entire congregation of the children of Israel and the foreigners who live among them will be forgiven, because all the people were ignorant. And if one person sins in ignorance, he is to offer a year-old goat as a sin–offering. The priest will atone for the person who erred by sinning in ignorance before the Eternal. He will atone for him, and he will be forgiven. You are to have one law for the native among the children of Israel and for the foreigner who lives among you, for acting in ignorance. But the person, the native or the foreigner, who acts with a high hand, who insults the Eternal, that person will be cut off from among his people, because he has despised the word of the Eternal and has violated his commandments. That person must be cut off. His sin is upon him.

Numbers 15:22–31

◇   ◇   ◇

*T*he man (who desecrated the Sabbath) must die. The entire congregation is to stone him outside the camp.

Numbers 15:35

◇   ◇   ◇

*S*peak to the children of Israel and say to them: Make fringes for yourselves on the corners of your garments, throughout your generations. Put a blue thread on the corner fringes. They will be for you a reminder. You will see them, and you will remember all of the Eternal's commandments and do them. And you will not seek after that which your heart and your eyes may solicit. Therefore, you are to remember and do all of my commandments; and you are to be sanctified to your God. I am the Eternal your God who brought you out from the land of Egypt to be your God. I am the Eternal your God.

Numbers 15:38–41

*S*eparate yourselves from among this congregation. I will consume them immediately.

Numbers 16:21

*S*peak to the congregation, saying: Ascend from around the dwelling of Korach, Dathan, and Abiram.

Numbers 16:24

*T*ell Eleazar, son of Aaron the priest, to raise the censers from within the conflagration and scatter the fire beyond, because they (the censers) are sanctified. From the censers of these sinners against their own souls you are to make flattened sheets, an overlaying for the altar, because they offered them before the Eternal. They are sanctified. They are to be as a sign for the children of Israel.

Numbers 17:2–3

*R*aise yourselves from among this congregation. I will consume them immediately.

Numbers 17:10

◇ ◇ ◇

*S*peak to the children of Israel, and take a staff from each father's house, from each of the leaders of the houses of their fathers—twelve staffs. Write each man's name on his staff, and write Aaron's name on the staff of Levi, because one staff is for each head of his father's house. Place them (the staffs) in the tent of meeting, before the testimony, where I meet with you. Indeed, the man whom I choose, his staff will blossom. I will halt the complaints of the children of Israel which they make to me against you.

Numbers 17:17–20

◇ ◇ ◇

*R*estore Aaron's staff before the testimony for observation as a sign for the sons of rebellion. And stop their complaints against me that they not die.

Numbers 17:25

*Y*ou, and your sons, and the house of your father with you are to bear the iniquity of the sanctuary. And you and your sons with you are to bear the iniquity of your priesthood. And also, your brothers, the tribe of Levi, the tribe of your father, are to approach with you, accompany you, and officiate for you; while you and your sons with you are before the tent of the testimony. They are to safeguard your observance and the observance of the whole tent; but they are not to approach the utensils of the sanctuary or the altar, that they, also you, not die. They are to accompany you and safeguard the observance of the tent of meeting for all of the service of the tent, but a stranger is not to approach you. You are to safeguard the observance of holiness and the observance of the altar, so no more anger will be upon the children of Israel. And here, I have taken your brothers, the Levites, from among the children of Israel—a gift granted to you by the Eternal, to perform the service of the tent of meeting. But you and your sons with you are to safeguard your priesthood concerning everything of the altar and within the veil. You are to serve; I have granted your priesthood as a gift of service. Therefore, the stranger who approaches will die.

Numbers 18:1–7

*A*nd here, I have granted you the observance of my raised–offerings. With all the sanctifications of the children of Israel, I have granted them to you and to your sons for anointing as an everlasting decree. This is to be yours from the holiest of holies, from the fire—all of their (the people's) offerings: all of their meal–offerings, all of their sin–offerings, and all of their guilt–offerings which they will render to me. It (the offering) is the holiest of holies for you and for your sons. You are to eat it in the holy of holies. Every male may eat it. It will be holy for you. Also, this is yours—their gift of a raised–offering along with every wave–offering of the children of Israel. I have given them to you, to your sons, and to your daughters with you as an everlasting decree. Anyone pure in your house may eat it. I have given you all the best oil and all the best wine and corn, their first-fruits which they are to give for the Eternal. The first-fruit of all which is in their land, which they are to bring for the Eternal, is to be yours. Anyone pure in your house may eat it. Everything forfeited in Israel is to be yours. Every firstling of a womb of all flesh which they offer for the Eternal, man and beast, is to be yours. But you must redeem the firstborn of man, and you are to redeem the firstborn of an impure beast. For its redemption you are to redeem it from a month old by your assessment—five shekels silver in the holy shekel, which is twenty pennyweights. But you are not to redeem the firstborn of an ox, the firstborn of a sheep, or the firstborn of a goat. They are holy. You are to sprinkle their blood over the altar and incinerate their fat as a fire–offering, a pleasing aroma for the Eternal. And their meat is to be yours as the breast of the wave–offering and the right shank is to be yours. All of the raised–offerings of the sanctifications which the children of Israel are to raise for the Eternal, I have given to you, to your sons, and to your daughters with you as an everlasting decree. It is an everlasting covenant of salt before the Eternal for you and for your descendants with you.

Numbers 18:8–19

You are not to inherit in their land, and you are not to have a portion among them. I am your portion and your inheritance among the children of Israel. Hence, to the children of Levi, I now give every tithe in Israel as an inheritance in exchange for their service which they perform, the service of the tent of meeting. Therefore, the children of Israel, bearing sin, are to approach no more to the tent of meeting, lest they die. The Levites are to perform the service of the tent of meeting, and they are to bear their iniquity. As an everlasting decree throughout your generations, they are not to receive an inheritance among the children of Israel; because I will give the tithe of the children of Israel, which they raise for the Eternal as a raised–offering, to the Levites as an inheritance. Therefore, I have said to them: They will not receive an inheritance among the children of Israel.

Numbers 18:20–24

And you are to speak to the Levites and say to them: When you take the tithe from the children of Israel which I have given to you from them as your inheritance, you are to raise a raised–offering for the Eternal from it, a tithe from the tithe. Your raised–offering will be considered for you as the corn from the mill and as the fullness from the winery. Hence, also you are to raise the Eternal's raised–offering from every tithe which you have taken from the children of Israel. You are to give the Eternal's raised–offering from it to Aaron the priest. From each of your gifts, you are to raise the best and the holiest for every raised–offering for the Eternal. And you are to say to them (the Levites): When you raise its best from it, it is to be considered for the Levites as the produce of the mill and as the produce of the winery. You may eat it anywhere, you and your household, because it is your wage in exchange for your service in the tent of meeting. Thereby, you will not bear sin on account of it when you raise its best from it. And you will not profane the sanctifications of the children of Israel, and you will not die.

Numbers 18:26–32

*T*his is the decree of the law which the Eternal has commanded, saying: Tell the children of Israel to bring you an unblemished red cow which has no deformity in it and over which no yoke was raised. You are to give it to Eleazar the priest. He is to take it outside the camp. It is to be slaughtered before him. Eleazar the priest is to take some of its blood with his finger and splash its blood seven times opposite the front of the tent of meeting. The cow is to be burned before his eyes. He is to burn its skin, its meat, its blood, and its excrement. The priest is to take cedar wood, hyssop, crimson-scarlet and throw them into the middle of the burning cow. The priest is to wash his garments, bathe his flesh in water; and afterwards, he is to enter the camp. The priest will be impure until the evening. And he who burns it (the cow) is to wash his garments in water, bathe his flesh in water, and be impure until the evening. A pure man is to gather the cow's ash and leave it outside the camp in a pure place. It is to be for the congregation of the children of Israel an observance of the cleansing water. It is an expiation–offering. The gatherer of the ash of the cow is to wash his garments and be impure until the evening. It will be for the children of Israel and for the foreigner who lives among them as an everlasting decree.

Numbers 19:2–10

*H*e who touches the corpse of any man will be rendered impure for seven days. He is to expiate himself on the third day, and on the seventh day he is to be considered pure. But if he does not expiate himself on the third day, then he will not be considered pure on the seventh day. Anyone who touches the dead, the corpse of a man who has died, and does not expiate himself makes the sanctuary of the Eternal impure. That soul will be cut off from Israel, because the cleansing water has not been sprinkled over him. He will be declared impure. His impurity is still upon him.

Numbers 19:11–13

*T*his is the law of a man who dies in a tent. All who come into the tent and all who are in the tent will be rendered impure for seven days. And every open vessel which does not have a lid bound over it is rendered impure. And in an open field, all who touch the sword-slain, the dead, the bone of a man, or a grave will be rendered impure for seven days. For the impure, they (the priests) are to take from the ash of the burnt expiation–offering and pour running water over it into a vessel. A pure man is to take hyssop, dip it in the water, and splash it on the tent, on all the vessels, on all the persons who were there, and on him who touched a bone, the slain, the dead, or a grave. The pure man is to splash the impure man on the third day and on the seventh day. He will be expiated on the seventh day. He will wash his clothes, bathe in water, and be declared pure in the evening. But the man who becomes impure and does not expiate himself, that soul will be cut off from among the assembly because he has defiled the sanctuary of the Eternal. The cleansing water has not been sprinkled over him. He is impure. It will be for them (the children of Israel) as an everlasting decree. The sprinkler of the cleansing water is to wash his clothes. He who touches the cleansing water will be rendered impure until the evening. And anything the impure man touches will be rendered impure. And the person who touches him will be rendered impure until the evening.

Numbers 19:14–22

*T*ake the staff; and you and Aaron your brother assemble the congregation. Speak to the rock before their eyes, and it will give its waters. Take water out of the rock for them, and let the congregation and their cattle drink.

Numbers 20:8

*B*ecause you did not believe in me, nor did you sanctify me in the eyes of the children of Israel, you will not bring this assembly into the land which I have given to them.

Numbers 20:12

*A*aron will be gathered to his people. He will not come to the land which I have given to the children of Israel, because both of you disobeyed me over the waters of Meriva. Take Aaron and Eleazar, his son, and let them ascend Mount Hor. Strip Aaron of his garments, and let Eleazar, his son, wear them. And Aaron will be gathered (unto his fathers) and die there.

Numbers 20:24–26

*M*ake a (copper) serpent for yourself, and put it on a flagstaff. It will be for anyone who is bitten so that he may see it and live.

Numbers 21:8

*G*ather the people. I will give them water.

Numbers 21:16

*D*o not fear him (Og, the King of Bashan), because I have given him, all of his people, and his land into your hand. Do to him just as you have done to Sichon, King of the Amorites who settled in Cheshbon.

Numbers 21:34

*W*ho are these people with you?

Numbers 22:9

*D*o not go with them (the officers of Balak). Do not curse the nation (Israel), because it is blessed.

Numbers 22:12

*I*f the men (the officers of Balak) come to call on you, rise. Go with them. But only do what I tell you to do.

Numbers 22:20

*W*hy did you strike your donkey these three times? Here I went out as a hinderer, because your way is contrary to mine; but the donkey saw me and turned from me three times. Unless it had turned from me, surely now, I would have killed you and let it live.

Numbers 22:32–33

◇   ◇   ◇

Go with the men (the officers of Balak), but only say what I tell you to say.

Numbers 22:35

◇   ◇   ◇

Return to Balak, and speak so.

Numbers 23:5

◇   ◇   ◇

Return to Balak, and speak so.

Numbers 23:16

◇   ◇   ◇

Take all the heads of the people (who worshipped Peor) and hang them—for the Eternal—facing the sun. The Eternal's raging anger will turn away from Israel.

Numbers 25:4

◇   ◇   ◇

Pinchas son of Eleazar, son of Aaron the priest, turned my wrath away from the children of Israel by being zealous in accordance with my jealousy among them. Hence, I did not annihilate the children of Israel because of my jealousy. Therefore say: Here, I give him my contract of peace. It will be for him and for his descendants after him as an everlasting contract of priesthood because he was zealous for his God and atoned for the children of Israel.

Numbers 25:11–13

◇   ◇   ◇

Be hostile to the Midianites and strike them; because they were hostile to you in their deceit, when they deceived you regarding Peor and

regarding Cozbi, daughter of a prince of Midian, their (the Midianites')
sister, who was struck down on the day of the plague because of Peor.

Numbers 25:17–18

*T*ake the census of the entire congregation of Israel from twenty
years of age and upward according to the house of their fathers, all who go
out to the army in Israel.

Numbers 26:2

*Y*ou are to partition the land as an inheritance for these (the
twelve tribes) by the number of names. For the many, you are to increase
their inheritance; and for the few, you are to decrease their inheritance. You
are to give each its inheritance according to its numbers. However, you are
to partition the land by lottery. They are to inherit by the names of their
fathers' tribes. You are to partition their inheritance among the many and
the few, according to the lottery.

Numbers 26:53–56

*T*hey must die in the desert.

Numbers 26:65

◇ ◇ ◇

*T*he daughters of Zelophechad speak correctly. You must give
them a portion of an inheritance from their fathers' brothers. You are to let
the inheritance of their fathers pass on to them. Therefore, speak to the
children of Israel, saying: If a man dies but has no son, you are to let his
inheritance pass on to his daughter. And if he has no daughter, give his
inheritance to his brothers. And if he has no brothers, give his inheritance
to his father's brothers. And if his father has no brothers, give his inheritance to his closest relative in his family; and he will keep it. It will be for
the children of Israel as a decree of judgment, just as the Eternal commanded Moses.

Numbers 27:7–11

Ascend this mountain of passages and see the land which I have given to the children of Israel. You will see it; and then you will be gathered to your people, as Aaron your brother was gathered, for disobeying me in the desert of Zin, in the dispute of the congregation—to sanctify me with water before their eyes. They are the waters of Meriva–Kadesh, desert of Zin.

Numbers 27:12–14

◇　◇　◇

Take Joshua son of Nun, a man of spirit, unto you and lay your hand on him. Stand him before Eleazar the priest and before all of the congregation, and command him before their eyes. Put your glory on him, so that the entire congregation of Israel listens. He is to stand before Eleazar the priest, and he is to ask him for the judgment of the Urim before the Eternal. According to it, they (the children of Israel) are to leave (the camp), and according to it, they are to encamp, he (Joshua) and all the children of Israel with him, the entire congregation.

Numbers 27:18–21

◇　◇　◇

Command the children of Israel and say to them: Be careful to offer me my offering, my bread for a fire–offering, a pleasing aroma, in its season. And say to them: This is the fire–offering that you are to offer to the Eternal: two unblemished year-old lambs per day, a continual ascension–offering. Prepare the first lamb in the morning, and prepare the second lamb at twilight, and a tenth of a bushel of flour mixed in a quarter gallon of pressed oil for a meal–offering. The continual ascension–offering, as prepared on Mount Sinai, is for a pleasing aroma, a fire–offering for the Eternal. And its libation: a quarter gallon for the first lamb, poured on the sanctification, an intoxicating libation for the Eternal. And you are to prepare the second lamb at twilight. Prepare it with the morning meal–offering and with its libation, a fire–offering, a pleasing aroma for the Eternal. And on the Sabbath day: two unblemished year-old lambs, two tenths of flour mixed in oil as a meal–offering, and its libation—the Sabbath ascension–offering on its Sabbath, with the continual ascension–offering and its libation. And at the beginnings of your months, you are to offer an ascension–offering for the Eternal: two young bulls, one ram, and seven unblemished year-old lambs. And three tenths of flour mixed in oil as a meal–offering for each bull. And two tenths of flour mixed in oil for each ram. And a tenth, a tenth of flour mixed in oil as a meal–offering for each lamb, an ascension–offering, a pleasing aroma, a fire–offering for the Eternal. And their libations: a half gallon of wine for the bull, a third of a gallon for the ram, and a quarter of a gallon for the lamb. This is the monthly ascension–offering in its month, for the months of the year. Also, one kid–goat is to be prepared as a sin–offering for the Eternal in addition to the continual ascension–offering and its libation. And in the first month, on the fourteenth day of the month is the Passover for the Eternal. And on the fifteenth day of this month is a holiday. Unleavened bread is to be eaten for seven days. On the first day there is to be a holy calling. Do not work at all. Offer a fire–offering, an ascension–offering for the Eternal: two young bulls, one ram, and seven year-old lambs. They are to be unblem-ished for you. And their meal–offerings of flour mixed in oil. You are to prepare three tenths per bull and two tenths per ram. Prepare a tenth, a tenth for each lamb, for the seven lambs, and one goat as a sin–offering to atone for you. Prepare these besides the morning ascension–offering which is for the continual ascension–offering. Likewise, you are to prepare the bread of a fire–offering each day, for seven days, a pleasing aroma for the Eternal. It is to be prepared with the continual ascension–offering and its libation. And on the seventh day, you are to have a holy calling. Do not work at all. And on the day of the first-fruits, when you offer a new offering for the Eternal, in your Feast of Weeks, you are to have a holy calling. Do not work at all. Offer an ascension–offering as a pleasing aroma for the Eternal: two young bulls, one ram, and seven year-old lambs. And their meal–offering of flour mixed in oil: three tenths for each bull, two tenths for the one ram, a tenth, a tenth for each lamb, for the seven lambs. And one goat–kid to atone for you. Prepare them besides the continual ascension–offering, its meal–offering, and their libations. They are to be unblemished for you.

Numbers 28:2–31

And in the seventh month, on the first of the month, you are to have a holy calling. Do not work at all. It is to be a day of trumpeting for you. You are to prepare an ascension–offering as a pleasing aroma for the Eternal: one young bull, one ram, and seven unblemished year-old lambs. And their meal–offerings of flour mixed in oil: three tenths for the bull, two tenths for the ram, and one tenth for each lamb, for the seven lambs. And one goat–kid as a sin–offering to atone for you, besides the monthly ascension–offering and its meal–offering, the continual ascension–offering and its meal–offering, and their libations, as customary, as a pleasing aroma, a fire–offering, for the Eternal. And on the tenth of this seventh month, you are to have a holy calling. You are to humble your souls. Do not work at all. Offer an ascension–offering for the Eternal, a pleasing aroma: one young bull, one ram, and seven year-old lambs. They are to be unblemished for you. And their meal–offering of flour mixed in oil: three tenths for the bull, two tenths for each ram, and a tenth, a tenth for each lamb, for the seven lambs. And one goat–kid as a sin–offering, besides the sin–offering of the atonements, the continual ascension–offering, their meal–offering, and their libations. And on the fifteenth day of the seventh month, you are to have a holy calling. Do not work at all. For seven days, you are to celebrate a holiday for the Eternal. Offer an ascension–offering, a fire–offering, a pleasing aroma for the Eternal: thirteen young bulls, two rams, and fourteen year-old lambs. They are to be unblemished. And their meal–offering of flour mixed in oil: three tenths for each bull, for the thirteen bulls; two tenths for each ram, for the two rams; and a tenth, a tenth for each lamb, for the fourteen lambs. And one goat–kid as a sin–offering, besides the continual ascension–offering, its meal–offering, and its libation. And on the second day: twelve young bulls, two rams, fourteen unblemished year-old lambs, their meal–offering, and their libations for the bulls, for the rams, and for the lambs, by their number, as customary, and one goat–kid as a sin–offering, besides the continual ascension–offering, its meal–offering, and their libations. And on the third day: eleven young bulls, two rams, fourteen unblemished year-old lambs, their meal–offering, and their libations for the bulls, for the rams, and for the lambs, by their numbers, as customary, and one goat as a sin–offering, besides the continual ascension–offering, its meal–offering, and its libation. And on the fourth day: ten bulls, two rams, fourteen unblemished year-old lambs, their meal–offering, and their libations for the bulls, for the rams, and for the lambs, by their numbers, as customary, and one goat–kid as a sin–offering, besides the continual ascension–offering, its meal–offering, and its libation. And on the fifth day: nine bulls, two rams, fourteen unblemished year-old lambs, their meal–offering, and their libations for the bulls, for the rams, and for the lambs, by their numbers, as customary, and one goat as a sin–offering, besides the continual ascension–offering, its meal–offering, and its libation. And on the sixth day: eight bulls, two rams, fourteen unblemished year-old lambs, their meal–offering, and their libations for the bulls, for the rams, and for the lambs, by their numbers, as customary, and one goat as a sin–offering, besides the continual ascension–offering, its meal–offering, and its libation. And on the seventh day: seven bulls, two rams, fourteen unblemished year-old lambs, their meal–offering, and their libations for the bulls, for the rams, and for the lambs, by their numbers, by their judgments, and one goat as a sin–offering, besides the continual ascension–offering, its meal–offering, and its libation. On the eighth day, you are to have a convocation. Do not work at all. Offer an ascension–offering, a fire–offering, a pleasing aroma for the Eternal: one bull, one ram, seven unblemished year-old lambs, their meal–offering, and their libations for the bull, for the ram, and for the lambs, by their numbers, as customary, and one goat as a sin–offering, besides the continual ascension–offering, its meal–offering, and its libation. Prepare these for the Eternal, in their seasons, aside from your vow–offerings and your contributions, for your ascension–offerings, for your meal–offerings, for your libations, and for your peace–offerings.

Numbers 29:1–39

*Y*ou must avenge the children of Israel against the Midianites. Afterwards, you will be gathered to your people.

Numbers 31:2

*Y*ou, and Eleazar the priest, and the leaders of the congregation, take the census of the captured spoils, man and beast, and split the spoils among the supporters of the war who went out with the army and among all of the congregation. Raise a tribute for the Eternal from the men of war who went out with the army: one from every five hundred men, cattle, donkeys, and sheep. Take from their half and give it to Eleazar the priest, a raised–offering for the Eternal. And from the half of the children of Israel, take one portion per fifty of the men, the cattle, the donkeys, the sheep, all the beasts and give them to the Levites, the guardians of the observance of the Eternal's tabernacle.

Numbers 31:26–30

*S*peak to the children of Israel and say to them: When you cross the Jordan to the land of Canaan, you are to drive out all of the settlers of the land from before you. You are to destroy all of their stone idols. You are to destroy all of their molten images. You are to demolish all of their altars. You are to possess the land and settle in it, because I have given the land to you, to possess it. You are to inherit the land by lottery, according to your families. For the many, you are to increase their inheritance; for the few, you are to decrease their inheritance. As it comes out for them, there is to be their lot. You are to inherit by your fathers' tribes. But if you do not drive the settlers of the land from before you, those remaining will be as prickles in your eyes and as thorns in your sides. They will distress you on the land in which you settle, and I will do to you just as I had thought to do to them.

Numbers 33:51–56

◇ ◇ ◇

Command the children of Israel and say to them: When you come to the land of Canaan, this is the land which will fall to you as an inheritance, the land of Canaan by its borders: The southern edge will be yours from the desert of Zin, near to Edom. It will be a southern border for you to the extremity of the Salt Sea, eastward. The border will encompass for you southward to the ascent of Akrabbim and pass to Zin. Its frontier will be southward to Kadesh–Barnea. It will go to Chazar–Adar and pass to Atzmon. The border will encompass from Atzmon to the Valley of Egypt, and its frontier will be the sea. And the western border will be for you the Great Sea and its borders. This will be the western border for you. And this will be the northern border for you. You are to draw, for yourselves, from the Great Sea to Mount Hor. You are to draw from Mount Hor to the out-set of Chamath. The frontier of the border will be to Tzedad. The border will pass to Ziphron. Its frontier will be Chatzar Einan. This will be the northern border for you. You are to turn, for yourselves, for the eastern border, from Chatzar Einan to Shepham. The border will descend from Shepham to Riblah, eastward of Ayin. The border will descend and touch on the shoulder of the Sea of Kinneret, eastward. The border will descend to the Jordan. Its frontier will be the Salt Sea. This will be your land, according to its surrounding borders.

Numbers 34:2–12

◇ ◇ ◇

These are the names of the men who are to inherit the land for you: Eleazar the priest and Joshua son of Nun. You are to take one leader from each tribe to inherit the land. And these are the names of the men: For the tribe of Judah, Caleb son of Jephunneh; and for the tribe of the sons of Simeon, Samuel son of Ammihud; and for the tribe of Benjamin, Elidad son

of Kislon; and a leader for the tribe of the sons of Dan, Buki son of
Yagli; for the sons of Joseph, a leader for the tribe of the sons of Menashe,
Hanniel son of Ephod; and a leader for the tribe of the sons of Ephraim,
Kemuel son of Shiphtan; and a leader for the tribe of the sons of
Zebulun, Elitzaphan son of Parnach; and a leader for the tribe of the sons
of Issachar, Paltiel son of Azzan; and a leader for the tribe of the sons of
Asher, Achihud son of Shelomi; and a leader for the sons of the tribe of
Naphtali, Pedahel son of Ammihud. These are the ones whom the Eternal
has commanded to inherit for the children of Israel in the land of Canaan.

Numbers 34:17–29

Command the children of Israel to give cities from the inheritance of their portion to the Levites to settle. And you are to give the
grounds surrounding the cities to the Levites. The cities are to be for them
to settle, and their grounds will be for their beasts, for their resources, and
for their livelihood. And the grounds of the cities which you are to give to
the Levites are from the wall of the city and outwards, a thousand forearms
around. You are to measure from outside the city, the eastern edge, two
thousand forearms; and the southern edge, two thousand forearms; and the
western edge, two thousand forearms; and the northern edge, two thousand
forearms, so the city is in the middle. This is to be the grounds of the cities
for them. And the cities which you are to give to the Levites are to be the
six cities of refuge which you are to give for the murderer to flee to. And
you are to give forty-two additional cities to them. All of the cities which
you are to give to the Levites are forty-eight cities and their grounds. Of
the cities which you are to give from the portion of the children of Israel,
from the many you are to increase; and from the few you are to decrease.
Each one (tribe) is to give from its cities to the Levites according to its
inheritance which it receives.

Numbers 35:2–8

Speak to the children of Israel and say to them: When you cross
the Jordan to the land of Canaan, prepare cities for yourselves to be your
cities of refuge; so the murderer, striking a person unintentionally, may flee
there. The cities will be for you for refuge from an avenger, so the murderer
will not die until he stands before the congregation for judgment. And the
cities which you are to give are to be six cities of refuge for you. You are

to give three of the cities before crossing the Jordan, and you are to give three of the cities in the land of Canaan, to be cities of refuge. These six cities are to be for the children of Israel, for the foreigner, and for the settler in their midst, for refuge, to flee there—anyone striking a person unintentionally. Yet, if he strikes him with an iron instrument and he dies, he is a murderer. The murderer must die. And if he strikes with a hand-stone by which he may die and he dies, he is a murderer. The murderer must die. Or, if he strikes with a wooden hand-instrument by which he may die and he dies, he is a murderer. The murderer must die. The avenger of blood may kill the murderer. He may kill him when he meets him. Therefore, if he (the aggressor) pushes him with hatred or hurls at him with malice and he dies, or he strikes him with his hand, with enmity, and he dies, the striker must die. He is a murderer. The avenger of blood may kill the murderer when he meets him. But if he (the aggressor) pushes him suddenly, without enmity, or he hurls any instrument on him without malice or any stone by which he may die without seeing, and it falls on him and he dies, but he is not an enemy to him and does not seek his harm, the congregation is to judge between the striker and the avenger of blood, according to these judgments. The congregation is to rescue the murderer from the hand of the avenger of blood. The congregation is to return him to his city of refuge where he has fled. He is to dwell in it until the death of the High Priest who has been anointed with the sanctified oil. But if the murderer goes beyond the border of his city of refuge where he has fled, and the avenger of blood finds him outside the border of his city of refuge, and the avenger of blood murders the murderer, no blood is on him, because he (the murderer) was to dwell in his city of refuge until the death of the High Priest. And after the death of the High Priest, the murderer is to return to the land of his portion. These are to be for you as a decree of judgment throughout your generations in all of your settlements. Anyone who strikes a person, according to witnesses—the murderer will be murdered. But one witness may not testify against a person for execution. And you may not take ransom for a murderer's life; whoever is guilty of killing must die. And you are not to take ransom for him who has fled to the city of his refuge to return to settle in the land—until the death of the priest. Hence, you are not to defile the land in which you live, because the blood defiles the land; and for the land, there is no atonement for the blood spilled upon it except with the blood of the spiller. Therefore, do not defile the land in which you settle, within which I dwell. For I, the Eternal, dwell among the children of Israel.

Numbers 35:10–34

DEUTERONOMY

*N*ow your days approach to die. Call Joshua and station yourselves in the tent of meeting. I will command him.

Deuteronomy 31:14

◇ ◇ ◇

*N*ow that you will lie with your fathers, these people will rise and
solicit the gods of the aliens of the land into which they enter. They will
abandon me and annul my contract which I have made with them. On that
day, my anger will rage against them. I will abandon them. I will hide my
face from them. They will be for devouring. Many evils and troubles will
find them. They will say on that day: Have these evils not found me
because my God is not among me? Indeed, I will hide my face on that day,
because of all the evils which they did; because they turned to other gods.
Therefore write this song for yourselves and teach it to the children of
Israel. Put it in their mouths, so that this song will be a witness for me
against the children of Israel. When I bring them to the land flowing with
milk and honey which I swore to their fathers, and they eat, and they are
satisfied, and they become fat, they will turn to other gods and serve them;
they will insult me and annul my contract. Yet, when many evils and
troubles find them, this song will testify before them; because it will not be
forgotten from the mouths of their descendants; for I know the inclination
which they prepare today even before I bring them into the land which I
have promised.

Deuteronomy 31:16–21

*B*e strong and bold, because you are to bring the children of Israel into the land which I promised them; and I will be with you.

Deuteronomy 31:23

◇   ◇   ◇

*A*scend this mountain of passages, Mount Nebo, which is in the land of Moab, which faces Jericho; and see the land of Canaan, which I give to the children of Israel as a portion. Die on the mountain, there where you ascend; and be gathered to your people, just as Aaron your brother died on Mount Hor and was gathered to his people, because you deceived me among the children of Israel by the waters of Meriva–Kadesh, desert of Zin, because you did not sanctify me among the children of Israel. Therefore, you will see the land from across, but you will not enter into the land which I give to the children of Israel.

Deuteronomy 32:49–52

◇   ◇   ◇

*T*his is the land which I have promised to Abraham, to Isaac, and to Jacob, saying: I will give it to your descendants. I have let you see it with your eyes, but you will not pass there.

Deuteronomy 34:4

INDEX A

TO WHOM GOD SPOKE

GENESIS

1:3–20	Himself	16:8–12	Hagar (by angel/ messenger)
1:22	infestations (fish) and fowl	17:1–2	Abram
1:24	Himself	17:4–8	Abram (Abraham)
1:26	Himself and the angels	17:9–21	Abraham
1:28–2:17	Man (male and female)	18:5–10	Abraham (by angel/ messenger)
2:18	Himself		
3:9–11	Man (Adam)	18:13	Abraham
3:13	Woman (Eve)	18:15	Sarah
3:14–15	serpent	18:17–19	Himself and the angels
3:16	Woman (Eve)	18:20–21	Abraham and the angels
3:17–19	Adam	18:26–32	Abraham
3:22	Himself	19:2–22	Lot (by angel/messenger)
4:6–15	Cain	20:3–7	Avimelech (in a dream)
6:3–7	Himself	21:12–13	Abraham
6:13–8:17	Noah	21:17–18	Hagar (by angel/ messenger)
8:21–22	Himself		
9:1–16	Noah and his sons	22:1–2	Abraham
9:17	Noah	22:11–18	Abraham (by angel/ messenger)
11:6–7	Himself		
12:1–3	Abram	25:23	Rebecca (by angel/ messenger)
12:7	Abram		
13:14–17	Abram	26:2–24	Isaac
15:1–4	Abram (in a vision)	28:13–15	Jacob
15:5–21	Abram	31:3	Jacob
		31:24	Laban (in a dream)

32:26–27	Jacob (by angel/ messenger)	32:29	Jacob (by angel/ messenger)
32:28	Jacob/Israel (by angel/ messenger)	35:1	Jacob
		35:10–12	Jacob (Israel)
		46:2–4	Israel (Jacob)

EXODUS

3:4–4:23	Moses	13:2	Moses
4:27	Aaron	13:17	Himself
6:1–7:5	Moses	14:2–26	Moses
7:9	Moses and Aaron	15:26	Moses and the people of Israel
7:14–9:5	Moses	16:4–19:24	Moses
9:8–9	Moses and Aaron	20:2–14	Moses and the people of Israel
9:13–11:9	Moses		
12:2–49	Moses and Aaron	20:19–40:15	Moses

LEVITICUS

1:2–8:3	Moses	13:1–59	Moses and Aaron
10:9–11	Aaron	14:2–32	Moses
11:2–47	Moses and Aaron	14:34–57	Moses and Aaron
12:2–8	Moses	15:2–33	Moses and Aaron
		16:2–27:33	Moses

NUMBERS

1:2–53	Moses	18:1–24	Aaron
2:2–31	Moses and Aaron	18:26–32	Moses
3:6–48	Moses	19:2–22	Moses and Aaron
4:2–20	Moses and Aaron	20:8	Moses
4:22–11:23	Moses	20:12–26	Moses and Aaron
12:4	Moses, Aaron, and Miriam	21:8–34	Moses
		22:9–20	Balaam (in a dream)
12:6–8	Aaron and Miriam	22:32–35	Balaam (by angel/ messenger)
12:14–14:25	Moses		
14:27–35	Moses and Aaron	23:5–16	Balaam
15:2–41	Moses	25:4–18	Moses
16:21	Moses and Aaron	26:2	Moses and Eleazar
16:24–17:25	Moses	26:53–35:34	Moses

DEUTERONOMY

31:14–21	Moses	32:49–52	Moses
31:23	Joshua	34:4	Moses

INDEX B

SUBJECT INDEX—CONCORDANCE

acquit	Exodus 23:6
admonish	Leviticus 19:2
adultery	Genesis 20:3, 20:6 Exodus 20:2 Leviticus 20:9 Numbers 5:12
adversely	Leviticus 26:14
afford	Leviticus 5:1, 12:2, 14:2, 25:25, 25:35, 27:2 Numbers 6:13
agate	Exodus 28:15
Aholiab	Exodus 31:2
albinism	Leviticus 13:38
alien	Leviticus 22:18 Deuteronomy 31:16
almond	Exodus 25:31
alone	Genesis 2:18 Exodus 24:1 Leviticus 13:38 Numbers 11:16
altar	Genesis 35:1 Exodus 20:19, 21:12, 27:1, 28:36, 29:10, 29:15, 29:19, 29:22, 29:29, 29:38, 30:1, 30:18, 30:23, 31:2, 34:10, 40:2 Leviticus 1:2, 1:10, 1:14, 2:1, 2:4, 2:11, 3:1, 3:6, 3:12, 4:2, 4:13, 4:22, 4:27, 5:1, 6:2, 6:7, 7:1, 7:29, 14:2, 16:2, 17:2, 17:8, 21:17, 22:18 Numbers 4:2, 4:22, 5:12, 7:11, 17:2, 18:1, 18:8, 33:51
Amalek	Exodus 17:14 Numbers 14:20
amen	Numbers 5:12
amend	Numbers 5:6
amethyst	Exodus 28:15
Amorite	Genesis 15:13, 15:18 Exodus 3:7, 3:16, 23:20, 33:1, 34:10 Numbers 21:34
anger	Genesis 3:14, 4:6, 6:7 Exodus 22:20, 32:9, 34:6 Leviticus 26:14 Numbers 1:49, 16:21, 18:1, 25:4, 25:11 Deuteronomy 31:16
annihilate	Genesis 18:20 Numbers 25:11
annul	Leviticus 26:14 Deuteronomy 31:16
anoint	Exodus 25:1, 28:36, 29:1, 29:19, 29:29, 30:23, 31:2, 40:2 Leviticus 2:4, 4:2, 4:13, 6:13, 7:11, 7:29, 8:2, 16:2, 21:1 Numbers 4:2, 6:13, 18:8, 35:10
appetite	Exodus 12:3

branch	Exodus 25:31 Leviticus 23:37

bread	Genesis 3:17
	Exodus 12:3, 16:4, 16:12, 16:28, 23:14, 23:20, 25:23, 29:1,
	    29:22, 29:29, 34:18
	Leviticus 3:6, 3:12, 6:7, 7:11, 8:2, 21:1, 21:17, 22:2, 22:18,
	    23:2, 23:10, 24:2, 26:3, 26:14
	Numbers 9:10, 15:2, 28:2

bread–offering	Numbers 4:2
break	Exodus 34:1, 34:10, 34:18 Leviticus 6:18, 11:24, 15:2, 24:14, 26:3, 26:14 Numbers 9:10
breast	Exodus 29:26 Leviticus 7:29 Numbers 6:13, 18:8
breastplate	Exodus 25:1, 28:1, 28:15, 29:1
breechcloth	Exodus 28:36 Leviticus 16:2
breed	Leviticus 19:19
bribe	Exodus 23:6
brook	Leviticus 23:37
brother	Genesis 4:9, 9:5, 16:11, 35:1 Exodus 4:14, 7:1, 28:1 Leviticus 16:2, 18:2, 19:2, 20:9, 21:1, 25:8, 25:25, 25:35, 26:14 Numbers 6:2, 8:24, 18:1, 20:8, 27:7, 27:12 Deuteronomy 32:49
bruised	Leviticus 22:18
bull	Exodus 9:1, 20:19, 21:33, 19:1, 29:10, 29:29 Leviticus 1:2, 4:2, 4:13, 8:2, 16:2, 23:10, 27:26 Numbers 8:6, 15:2, 15:22, 28:2, 29:1
burden	Exodus 6:2, 23:4 Numbers 4:2, 4:18, 4:22, 4:29, 11:16
burn	Exodus 12:3, 21:12 Leviticus 6:2, 6:18, 7:11, 13:47, 16:2, 19:2, 20:9, 21:1 Numbers 19:2
burn (medical)	Leviticus 13:18
bury	Genesis 15:13
buy	Leviticus 25:8, 25:29, 25:35
buzzard	Leviticus 11:2
Cain	Genesis 4:15
calamity	Exodus 21:12
Caleb	Numbers 14:20, 14:27, 34:17
calf	Exodus 32:7
calling	Leviticus 23:2, 23:10, 23:24, 23:27, 23:34, 23:37 Numbers 28:2, 29:1

	Leviticus 4:13, 4:22, 4:27, 5:1, 5:15, 5:21, 19:19 Numbers 14:20, 15:22
fork	Exodus 27:1 Numbers 4:2
forsworn	Numbers 5:12
fowl	Genesis 1:20, 1:22, 1:26, 1:28, 1:29, 6:7, 6:13, 7:1, 8:16, 9:1, 9:9 Leviticus 1:14, 7:23, 11:2, 11:39, 14:2, 14:34, 17:8, 20:9
frame	Exodus 25:23
frankincense	Exodus 30:34 Leviticus 2:1, 2:11, 5:1, 6:7, 24:2 Numbers 5:12
freedom	Exodus 21:1, 21:12 Leviticus 19:19
fringes	Numbers 15:38
frogs	Exodus 7:26, 8:1
fruit	Genesis 1:11, 1:29 Leviticus 19:19, 23:37, 25:8, 26:3, 26:14, 27:26
fruitful	Genesis 1:22, 1:28, 8:16, 9:1, 9:5, 17:4, 17:19, 35:11 Exodus 23:20 Leviticus 26:3
frying-pan	Leviticus 2:4, 6:13, 7:1
furnace	Exodus 9:8
Gad	Numbers 1:2, 2:2
game	Leviticus 17:8
garden	Genesis 2:16
garment	Exodus 22:4, 22:24, 28:1, 29:1, 29:19, 29:29, 31:2, 40:2 Leviticus 6:2, 6:18, 8:2, 11:24, 11:39, 13:1, 13:47, 14:34, 15:16, 16:2, 19:19, 21:1 Numbers 15:38, 19:2, 20:24
gate	Exodus 20:2, 27:9, 40:2 Numbers 4:22
generation	Genesis 7:1, 9:12, 15:13, 17:4, 17:9 Exodus 3:15, 12:3, 20:2, 27:20, 29:38, 30:1, 30:18, 30:23, 31:13, 34:6, 40:2 Leviticus 3:12, 6:7, 7:29, 10:9, 17:2, 21:17, 22:2, 23:10, 23:27, 23:37, 24:2, 25:29 Numbers 9:10, 10:2, 15:2, 15:18, 15:22, 15:38, 18:20, 35:10
Gershon	Numbers 4:22
gift	Exodus 28:36 Leviticus 23:37 Numbers 18:8, 18:26
gizzard	Leviticus 1:14
glorify	Leviticus 19:2, 19:19
glory	Exodus 28:1, 28:36 Numbers 14:20, 27:18

|---|---|
	Leviticus 14:34, 16:2, 17:2, 17:8, 22:2, 22:18, 25:29, 27:14 Numbers 1:2, 3:15, 4:2, 4:22, 4:29, 12:6, 17:17, 18:1, 18:8, 18:26, 26:2
humble	Leviticus 16:2, 23:27 Numbers 29:1
hunchback	Leviticus 21:17
hunt	Leviticus 17:8
Hur	Exodus 31:2
husband	Genesis 3:16, 20:3 Exodus 21:1, 21:12 Leviticus 21:1, 22:2 Numbers 5:12
husk	Numbers 6:2
hyssop	Leviticus 14:2, 14:34 Numbers 19:2, 19:14
idolatry	Exodus 20:2, 20:19, 34:10 Leviticus 19:2, 26:1, 26:14 Numbers 33:51
ignorance	Leviticus 4:2, 4:22, 4:27, 5:15, 22:2 Numbers 15:22
image	Genesis 1:26, 9:5 Exodus 20:2 Numbers 12:6, 33:51
impoverished	Leviticus 25:25,25:35
impure	Leviticus 5:1, 7:11, 10:9, 11:2, 11:24, 11:39, 12:2, 13:1, 13:9, 13:18, 13:29, 13:38, 13:47, 14:34, 15:2, 15:16, 16:2, 17:8, 18:2, 18:22, 19:19, 20:2, 20:9, 21:1, 22:2, 27:2, 27:26 Numbers 5:2, 5:12, 6:2, 9:10, 18:8, 19:2, 19:11, 19:14, 35:10
inauguration	Numbers 7:11
incense	Exodus 25:1, 30:1, 30:23, 30:34, 40:2 Leviticus 4:2, 16:2 Numbers 4:2
incest	Leviticus 18:2, 19:19, 20:9
incision	Leviticus 19:19, 21:1
inclination	Genesis 8:21 Deuteronomy 31:16
increase	Leviticus 19:19
incriminate	Leviticus 4:2, 4:13, 4:22, 4:27, 5:1, 5:15, 5:21
infection	Leviticus 13:1, 13:9, 13:18, 13:29, 13:38, 13:47, 14:2, 14:34
infestation	Leviticus 11:2, 11:39
ingathering	Exodus 23:14, 34:18
inhabitant	Exodus 23:20, 34:10 Leviticus 18:22, 25:8
inherit	Genesis 13:14, 15:4, 15:7, 17:4, 22:16, 35:11

power	Leviticus 26:14
praiseworthy	Leviticus 19:19
prayer	Genesis 20:6
predator	Exodus 8:16
presence	Exodus 25:1, 29:38, 33:14
prey	Numbers 14:27
price	Exodus 22:15 Leviticus 25:8
pricklers	Numbers 33:51
priest	Exodus 19:3, 19:21, 19:24, 28:1, 28:36, 29:1, 29:29, 29:38, 30:23, 31:2, 40:2 Leviticus 1:2, 1:10, 1:14, 2:1, 2:4, 2:11, 3:1, 3:6, 3:12, 4:2, 4:13, 4:22, 4:27, 5:1, 5:15, 5:21, 6:2, 6:13, 6:18, 7:1, 7:11, 7:29, 12:2, 13:1, 13:9, 13:18, 13:29, 13:38, 13:47, 14:2, 14:34, 15:2, 15:16, 16:2, 17:2, 19:19, 21:1, 21:17, 22:2, 23:10, 27:2, 27:14, 27:16 Numbers 3:6, 4:2, 4:22, 4:29, 5:6, 5:12, 6:13, 10:2, 15:22, 17:2, 18:1, 18:26, 19:2, 25:11, 27:18, 31:26, 34:17, 35:10
prince	Genesis 17:19 Numbers 25:17
principal	Leviticus 5:21 Numbers 5:6
profane	Leviticus 10:9, 18:2, 19:2, 20:2, 21:1, 21:17, 22:2, 22:27 Numbers 18:26
property	Exodus 22:4 Leviticus 25:8, 25:25, 25:29, 25:35, 27:16, 27:26
prophet	Genesis 20:6 Exodus 7:1 Numbers 12:6
prudent	Exodus 23:6
prune	Leviticus 19:19, 25:2
psoriasis	Leviticus 13:29, 14:34
pulpit	Leviticus 26:14
punish	Exodus 32:33, 34:6 Leviticus 18:22, 26:14
purchase	Leviticus 22:2, 25:35, 27:16
purple	Exodus 25:1, 26:1, 26:31, 27:9, 28:1, 28:6, 28:15, 28:31 Numbers 4:2
push	Numbers 35:10
quantity	Leviticus 19:19
quarantine	Leviticus 13:1, 13:9, 13:18, 13:29, 13:47, 14:34
quarrel	Exodus 21:12
rabbit	Leviticus 11:2

	Numbers 34:2
sanctification	Leviticus 5:15, 22:2, 27:26 Numbers 5:6, 18:8, 18:26, 28:2

sanctify	Exodus 13:2, 19:21, 20:2, 28:1, 28:36, 29:1, 29:19, 29:26,
	  29:29, 29:38, 30:23, 30:34, 31:2, 31:13, 40:2
	Leviticus 6:18, 11:39, 12:2, 14:2, 16:2, 19:19, 20:2, 20:9,
	  21:1, 21:17, 22:2, 22:27, 23:10, 24:2, 25:8, 27:2, 27:16,
	  27:26
	Numbers 3:12, 5:12, 6:2, 6:13, 8:6, 11:16, 15:38, 17:2, 20:12,
	  27:12, 35:10
	Deuteronomy 32:49

sanctuary	Exodus 25:1, 28:15, 28:31, 29:29 Leviticus 4:2, 6:18, 12:2, 16:2, 19:19, 20:2, 21:1, 21:17, 26:1, 26:14 Numbers 4:2, 4:18, 8:6, 18:1, 19:11, 19:14
sand	Genesis 22:16
sapphire	Exodus 28:15
Sarah	Genesis 16:8, 17:15, 17:19, 18:9, 18:10, 18:13, 21:12
satiety	Leviticus 25:8, 26:3, 26:14
satisfy	Exodus 16:12 Deuteronomy 31:16
save	Numbers 10:2
say (see speak)	
scale	Leviticus 11:2, 19:19
scar	Leviticus 13:18
scarlet	Exodus 25:1, 26:1, 26;31, 27:9, 28:1, 28:6, 28:15, 28:31 Leviticus 14:2, 14:34 Numbers 4:2, 19:2
scatter	Leviticus 26:14 Numbers 17:2
screen	Exodus 26:31, 27:9, 40:2 Numbers 4:2, 4:22
sea	Genesis 1:22, 1:26, 1:28, 9:1, 22:16 Exodus 14:2, 14:15, 14:26, 20:2, 23:20 Leviticus 11:2 Numbers 34:2
sea gull	Leviticus 11:2
season	Genesis 1:14, 17:19, 18:13, 23:14 Leviticus 23:2 Numbers 9:2, 9:10, 28:2, 29:1
secret	Numbers 5:12
security	Leviticus 25:8, 26:3
seed	Genesis 1:11, 1:29, 3:14, 7:1 Leviticus 11:24, 26:14, 27;16, 27:26
sell	Exodus 21:1, 21:12, 21:33, 22:1 Leviticus 25:8, 25:25, 25:29, 25:35, 27:16, 27:26

silver	Exodus 3:16, 11:1, 21:28, 25:1, 26:15, 26:31, 27:9, 30:12, 31:2 Leviticus 5:15, 27:2, 27:14, 27:16 Numbers 3:45, 10:2, 18:8
Simeon	Numbers 1:2, 2:2, 34:17
sin	Genesis 4:6, 18:20, 20:6 Exodus 20:2, 23:20, 28:36, 32:33, 34:6 Leviticus 4:2, 4:13, 4:22, 4:27, 5:1, 5:15, 5:21, 7:11, 16:2, 19:2, 19:19, 20:9, 22:2, 24:14, 26:14 Numbers 5:6, 6:2, 9:10, 15:22, 17:2, 18:20, 18:26
sin—offering	Exodus 29:10, 29:29, 30:1 Leviticus 4:2, 4:13, 4:22, 4:27, 6:7, 6:18, 7:1, 7:29, 8:2, 12:2, 14:2, 15:2, 15:16, 16:2, 23:10 Numbers 6:2, 6:13, 8:6, 15:22, 18:8, 28:2, 29:1
Sinai	Exodus 19:10, 34:1 Leviticus 7:29 Numbers 28:2
sister	Leviticus 18:2, 20:9, 21:1 Numbers 6:2, 25:17
sit	Genesis 35:1 Exodus 16:28 Leviticus 13:38, 15:2, 15:16
skin	Exodus 22:24, 25:1, 26:7 Leviticus 1:2, 4:2, 7:1, 13:1, 13:18, 13:29, 13:38, 16:2 Numbers 8:6, 19:2
sky	Genesis 1:6, 1:14, 1:20
slain	Numbers 19:14
slander	Leviticus 19:2
slaughter	Exodus 21:33, 29:10, 29:15, 29:19, 34:18 Leviticus 1:2, 1:10, 3:1, 3:6, 3:12, 4:2, 4:13, 4:22, 4:27, 6:18, 7:1, 14:2, 14:34, 16:2, 17:2, 22:27 Numbers 19:2
slave (*see* servant)	
sleep	Genesis 19:2
slut	Leviticus 21:1
smell	Leviticus 26:14
snake (*see* serpent)	
Sodom	Genesis 18:20 thru 19:21
soldiers	Exodus 14:2, 14:15
solicit	Exodus 34:10 Leviticus 17:2, 19:19, 20:2, 21:1 Numbers 14:27, 15:38 Deuteronomy 31:16
son	Genesis 6:13, 8:16, 16:11, 17:15, 17:19, 18:10, 18:13, 19:12, 22:2, 22:12, 22:16 Exodus 3:16, 4:21, 10:1, 20:2, 21:1, 21:28, 22:27, 23:10,

unclean	Leviticus 5:1
uncover	Leviticus 18:2, 20:9
unleavened (*see* leaven)	
upright	Leviticus 26:3
Ur Kasdim	Genesis 15:7
Urim	Exodus 28:15 Numbers 27:18
utensil	Exodus 22:4, 25:1, 25:31, 27:1, 27:9, 30:23, 31:2, 40:2 Leviticus 6:18, 11:24, 13:47 Numbers 1:49, 3:6, 4:2, 4:22, 4:29, 18:1
vain	Exodus 20:2 Leviticus 26:14
valley	Genesis 19:17 Numbers 14:20, 34:2
value	Leviticus 5:15, 5:21
veil	Exodus 26:31, 27:20, 30:1, 31:2, 40:2 Leviticus 4:2, 4:13, 16:2, 21:17, 24:2 Numbers 4:2, 18:1
vessel	Exodus 3:16, 11:1 Leviticus 11:24, 14:2, 14:34, 15:2 Numbers 4:2, 5:12, 19:14
vest	Exodus 25:1, 28:1, 28:6, 28:15, 28:31, 29:1
village	Leviticus 25:29
vineyard	Exodus 22:4, 23:10 Leviticus 19:2, 25:2
vintage	Exodus 22:27 Leviticus 26:3
violate	Numbers 15:22
violence	Genesis 6:13, 16:11
virgin	Exodus 22:15 Leviticus 21:1
vision	Numbers 12:6
voice	Genesis 4:10, 21:12, 21:17, 22:16, 26:2 Exodus 3:16, 4:8, 15:26, 19:3, 23:20, 28:31 Leviticus 5:1 Numbers 14:20
voluntary–offering	Leviticus 7:11
vomit	Leviticus 18:22, 20:9
vow	Leviticus 22:18, 23:37, 27:2 Numbers 6:2, 6:13, 15:2
vow–offering	Leviticus 7:11 Numbers 29:1
vulture	Leviticus 11:2
wage	Leviticus 19:2